Bond
The secrets of Comprehension

Michellejoy Hughes

Nelson Thornes

Text © Michellejoy Hughes 2007
Original illustrations © Nelson Thornes Ltd 2007

The right of Michellejoy Hughes to be identified as author of this work has been asserted by her in accordance with the Copyright, Designs and Patents Act 1988.

All rights reserved. No part of this publication may be reproduced or transmitted in any form or by any means, electronic or mechanical, including photocopy, recording or any information storage and retrieval system, without permission in writing from the publisher or under licence from the Copyright Licensing Agency Limited, of Saffron House, 6–10 Kirby Street, London, EC1N 8TS.

Any person who commits any unauthorised act in relation to this publication may be liable to criminal prosecution and civil claims for damages.

Published in 2007 by:
Nelson Thornes Ltd
Delta Place
27 Bath Road
CHELTENHAM
GL53 7TH
United Kingdom

11 / 10 9 8 7 6 5 4

A catalogue record for this book is available from the British Library

ISBN 978 0 7487 8480 6

Illustrations by GreenGate Publishing Services and Peters and Zabransky Ltd
Page make-up by GreenGate Publishing Services, Tonbridge, Kent

Printed and bound in Croatia by Zrinski

Acknowledgements

The authors and publishers wish to thank the following for permission to use copyright material:

Extract from *The Lion, the Witch and the Wardrobe* by C S Lewis.
Copyright © 1950 C S Lewis Pte Ltd. Reprinted by permission.

'Hawk Roosting' by Ted Hughes from *New Selected Poems 1957–1994* reprinted by permission of the publisher, Faber and Faber Limited.

Every effort has been made to trace the copyright holders, but if any have been inadvertently overlooked the publishers will be pleased to make the necessary arrangements at the first opportunity.

Contents

A Introduction

1. Why do you need this book? — 1
2. How can you use this book? — 3
3. How is this book organised? — 3
4. What skills will your child need? — 4
5. How can you help? — 5

B Three steps to comprehension

1. Read and understand the text — 7
   - Find clues in the text — 7
   - Discover active reading — 8
   - Recognise different text types — 27

2. Understand the question — 38
   - Reorganise and select information — 39
   - Apply word knowledge and grammar — 47
   - Find, deduce and infer information — 58
   - Prepare a knowledge-based response — 65
   - Introduce personal opinion — 69
   - Compare texts — 77

3. Evaluate your work — 84
   - Write a good answer — 85
   - Avoid losing marks — 85
   - Assess your own answers — 86
   - Check your work — 96
   - Assess your speed — 99

C Appendices

1. Glossary — 103
2. Answers — 104
3. Additional resources — 110

Central pull-out section
Contains two of the three free test papers that accompany this book. Test 1 is available at www.bond11plus.co.uk. See page 4 for more details.

A Introduction

1 Why do you need this book?

Reading and understanding texts is a core skills area that all children have to learn from an early age because it forms a central part of exams that they will have to do throughout their school life. This book is an invaluable resource for all children from the beginning of Year 3 through to the end of Year 9 because it covers all the key comprehension requirements for the 11+, 12+ and 13+ Examinations, the Common Entrance Examination and the KS2 and KS3 English SATs. These exams are explained in more detail below. This book is also a useful manual that can support school-based learning and can provide additional help for anyone who wants to improve his or her comprehension skills.

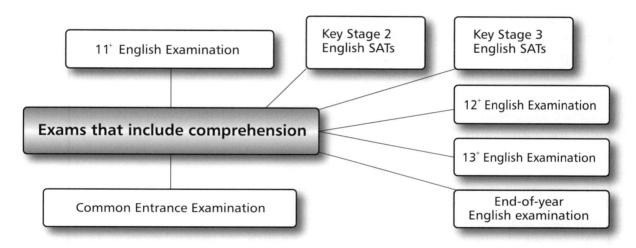

The **11+ Examination** is a test used by UK grammar schools and some selective secondary schools to assess the academic ability of pupils who are applying to join the school in the following September. An 11+ exam can test some or all of a child's English, maths, verbal reasoning and non-verbal reasoning skills in individual subject papers, which can be written in a standard or multiple-choice format.

Most 11+ English exams include at least one comprehension task, and some papers are completely based around a comprehension text. Children may be asked to answer questions that require them to find, select or reorganise information in the text and provide answers based on knowledge, interpretation or personal opinion. Responses may need to be presented in a range of formats, such as selection of the correct multiple-choice option, one word or a short phrase, a few lines or a more lengthy explanation written in several paragraphs. On average a child will have about 50 minutes to complete an English paper and the comprehension exercise could carry up to 100% of the total available marks. Sometimes the 11+ exam will have a section requiring simple comprehension answers and a more in-depth section requiring open-ended or more personal response answers.

The time of year when these exams are taken can differ from region to region, but most schools and LEAs set the exams between November and January. Always find out from a school when their exam is being set, what subjects are being tested and in what format the exam papers will be written. (More detailed guidance on the 11+ exam process and how to approach it can be found in *The Parents' Guide to the 11+* and *How to do ... 11+ English*, see Additional resources; page 110.)

The **12+ and 13+ Examinations** form part of the late transfer process for some grammar and selective secondary schools. These exams are used to assess the ability of a small number of pupils who may apply to join the school in Years 8 or 9. The format and skills tested are similar to those in the 11+, though the content is likely to be more advanced at this age.

Schools often set an English paper in these tests, which will include a comprehension exercise. As with the 11+, some schools may base the whole paper around a comprehension text. Question types and answer formats are likely to be the same as for the 11+ English exam (see above). On average a child will have about 50 minutes to complete an English paper and the comprehension exercise could carry up to 100% of the total available marks.

The **Common Entrance Examination (CEE)** is used by many independent schools to assess pupils who are transferring to a secondary school at the age of 11 or 13. The 11+ level exam is sat during the spring school term, whereas the 13+ level exam can be sat in either the spring or the summer term. The three core subjects of English, maths and science are tested at both entrance levels. A comprehension paper will usually be included for both exams. It is likely to carry 50% of the total English marks, may last from 40 minutes to 1 hour 15 minutes and could include more than one comprehension task.

Standard Attainment Tests (SATs) are the compulsory exams sat at the end of KS1, KS2 and KS3, although some schools do use optional SATs in other years. They are government set requirements that test pupils in English, maths and science. In the English SATs, the comprehension element is presented in the form of the Reading Test. At KS2, a pupil will have on average 15 minutes to read the reading booklet and 45 minutes to answer the questions. At KS3, a pupil will also have about 15 minutes to read the reading booklet and one hour to answer the questions.

For the KS2 and KS3 papers, children will be expected to find, select or reorganise information as required in order to find an answer and develop responses using knowledge and personal opinion. They need to be able to select an answer from multiple-choice options and to recognise when a question requires a brief or more detailed response or a more visual answer, such as a table.

End-of-year exams may be independently set by individual schools, but it is now quite common for schools to buy in government SATs for non-compulsory years (Years 3, 4, 5, 7 and 8). Whether a school uses their own end-of-year exams or uses SATs, there will usually be a comprehension test in the English paper. Pupils will often have a defined time to read the reading booklet and a further prescribed time to answer the questions. These exams are designed to test similar skills to the compulsory SATs papers and therefore include the same types of question and answer formats.

2 How can you use this book?

The secrets of Comprehension is a practical guide designed for use by children, but it features tips and advice for parents too. It makes clear the skills needed to succeed at comprehension tasks (whether practising for secondary school selection tests, SATs or other end-of-year exams) and highlights ways in which parents can help their children to strengthen these skills. This book is also full of practical exercises that cover all the main comprehension question types, and it offers help for all ages and abilities.

This key resource is part of the long-established Bond series, which continues to be used by many parents and tutors to help children prepare for the 11+ (or other selective entry exams), as well as to support SATs practice and general improvement. Using this workbook in conjunction with the other English resources in the series will help to provide a wide variety of practice for comprehension skills. Details of the full range of Bond English resources available are listed in the Additional resources section in Appendix C.

3 How is this book organised?

This book is divided into three main sections:

A *Introduction*
B *Three steps to comprehension*
C *Appendices*

Section A explains the stages when children are likely to face comprehension tests between Year 3 and Year 9, which skills will be tested in these exams, and how you can support and develop your child's ability.

Section B contains the core content of this book, taking children steadily through the three key steps necessary to improve comprehension skills.

- **1 Read and understand the text**
Here children learn how to find vital clues in an extract by identifying keywords, by asking themselves a set of core questions as they read and by thinking about the possible source of a text.

- **2 Understand the question**
This next step takes a detailed look at six of the most common question types that can appear on comprehension papers and the skills they test. Example questions in each of the six groups are worked through methodically using clear, step-by-step strategies that show the essential thought processes involved. Each question type is examined in relation to a different extract, and practice activities are included throughout to help reinforce the techniques that have been learned. Where the icon www appears next to an extract, it shows that the text is also available to download free from our web site. Visit www.bond11plus.co.uk and follow the Free Resources link.

- **3 Evaluate your work**
This section recaps on key strategies for creating good answers and for avoiding common pitfalls that can lead to lost marks. It also offers clear guidance for self-assessment and explores the importance of leaving sufficient time to check answers.

Section C provides details of the additional English resources you can use alongside this book, whether your child needs support for selective secondary school entrance exams, English SATs or improvement of basic English skills. Answers to all practice and test paper questions and a glossary of important terms are also included here.

This book is also accompanied by **three graded comprehension papers**. Test 1 is suitable for Key Stage 2 SATs preparation, as well as a warm-up exercise for secondary school entrance exams. Test 2 supports practice for 11+ English tests and the English paper that is set as part of the CEE. It can also be used for extended Key Stage 2 SATs preparation. Test 3 sets more challenging questions and is therefore ideal for supporting 12+ or 13+ English exam practice, as well as more advanced 11+ English work. All three tests are available to download free via the Free Resources link on the Bond web site, and hard copies of Tests 2 and 3 can also be found in the detachable central section of this book. If you wish to assess your child's progress, these tests can be set before and after working through this book.

4 What skills will your child need?

As we have seen, your child will have to sit a comprehension test at various points during his or her education, each of which may consist of different text types, genres or writing styles. These tests may be set at different difficulty levels but each task will be testing a similar set of skills. In all of these tests, examiners will be looking for children to display ability in key areas and to meet particular learning targets.

By the time of the 11+, your child will be expected to show that he or she can:

- *decode a text accurately*
- *develop information from given texts*
- *infer, interpret and deduce information from given texts*
- *comment on and identify a writer's purpose and viewpoint*
- *summarise part of a text*
- *recognise the overall effects a text has on the reader*
- *relate texts to their historical, cultural and social context*
- *understand, select, describe or retrieve information from given texts*
- *recognise, identify and comment on the organisation and structure of texts including grammatical and presentational features*
- *comment on or explain a writer's use of language, grammar and literary features*
- *display knowledge of vocabulary, spelling and syntax*
- *explain vocabulary in context*
- *understand sequence and order of events*
- *continue a piece of writing*
- *give a personal interpretation or opinion of a text*
- *give a prediction based on clues in a text*
- *support points with the use of quotations or textual referencing.*

These key skills are central to the 11⁺, 12⁺ and 13⁺ exams, and the KS2 and KS3 SATs, so it is important for your child to feel confident in every one of these areas. The ten active reading questions and six common question types explored in section B, are each linked to these key skills through a skills checklist. This will make it easier for you and your child to see where and how these skills can be tested in comprehension exercises and which techniques can help to develop these skills.

5 How can you help?

Before your child begins to look at this book, and while he or she works through it, there are many ways in which you can assist. The most vital way is to build reading skills, because these are the fundamental roots of comprehension. Here are the main types of reading skill that your child will need to develop in order to improve their performance in comprehension exams, and some suggestions for how you can support these skills.

Preparation reading will encourage your child to build up reading skills such as recognising keywords, understanding what examination questions require, learning how to interpret tables, facts and figures or other graphic forms of information. These skills can be built up well before the examination takes place with a range of everyday reading activities. For example:

- *How fast can your child find the sugar content from their breakfast cereal box?*
- *Does your child know how to follow a bus timetable?*
- *Can your child read a short story and recognise the keywords in it?*
- *Can your child take notes and annotate reading material?*

Productive reading will develop your child's ability to take in information with a first reading. So much emphasis is placed on reading for pleasure that we sometimes overlook reading for information; children can find themselves caught up in the reading and imagining without focusing on the detail of the text. This often means a rereading of the information is required to answer the questions and this wastes valuable time.

When your child has read a page, cover up the page and ask them to recall as much as they can. It is surprising how many children are completely lost when they cannot reread the information, so fine-tuning this technique is vital if your child is to save precious time in an exam environment.

Task reading is the reading that is done whilst bearing in mind the question or preparation reading requirements. It is reading whilst being fully focused on the task at hand and involves taking in the maximum amount of information in the one reading. This skill requires a child to:

- *hone in on the keywords*
- *grasp style and tone*
- *recognise features that may be asked about.*

As your child reads, encourage him or her to make notes, to highlight features that seem important and to underline individual words or sentences that may be relevant to the task.

Speed reading is not simply reading quickly, it is reading effectively. If your child can take in maximum information in minimal time, the answering of questions will be far easier. It is often the slow reader, or children who read without focus and understanding, who will perform worse in comprehension tests. It is important not to sacrifice quality of reading for speed though. Gradually building up the speed at which a child can effectively read is good preparation.

The root of this skill is actually encouraging your child to read as much as possible and to read with focus. Taking a paragraph at a time, allow your child to read and then recall what has been read. By highlighting the keywords in the paragraph and paying less attention to connective words, a child can reduce the information to its simplest form. It is the opposite process to a writer having the bare bones of a story and adding layers of meaning and description to create a piece of writing. Speed reading takes away the layers of meaning and description to go back to the bare bones of a piece of writing.

Checking forms the natural balance to task reading. While a child task reads by keeping the question in mind, checking is the continual process of ensuring an answer remains focused on the question. Many answers begin well but they then lose their direction and so lose marks. Children sometimes panic and think they should add everything into an answer, but maximum marks are available for a response that is tightly focused, succinct and does what the question asks. Encourage your child not only to check his or her answers at the end, but also during the answering process to keep on track.

Word knowledge is a vital element of all comprehension exams. Typical questions include knowing the meaning of a specific word or phrase, recognising correctly spelt words and sometimes defining common sayings or proverbs. Developing a high standard of vocabulary will help to underpin several comprehension question types. You can support this by providing as many opportunities as possible for your child to expand their word knowledge. *Schonell's Essential Spelling* series is an excellent starting point and *How to do ... 11+ English* also has a wealth of ideas and activities for encouraging reading and spelling skills. (See the Additional resources section in Appendix C for more details.)

Developing comprehension skills is most effectively achieved by reading as often as possible and as wide a variety of texts as possible. Encouraging children to do this will help them extend their vocabulary, gain a stronger understanding of words and develop their own responses to, and opinions of, texts. Creating the right environment for this is crucial. When your child has finished reading a book, ask them questions about it: *Did they enjoy it? What did they enjoy the most? How effective was the author?* When they have finished reading a chapter or section, ask questions: *What has happened so far? How do they think it will continue or a problem will be resolved? In what ways might the author take the character or plot forward?*

> ✓ **Parent Tip**
>
> *Reading can be insular, so share your reading with your child. Whether it is a magazine, newspaper, novel or poem, if you vocalise your ideas and opinions you will help your child to vocalise theirs. Explain why you did or didn't enjoy what you have read and how you think the writer has dealt with a plot or a character. Even basic opinions such as, "I like this book because..." are a start!*

It is never too late to help your child towards better comprehension skills. Many of the ideas offered here will strengthen not only comprehension skills, but also other key literacy areas, ensuring your child has the best possible support in school.

As comprehension skills underpin many other subjects, success in this area can affect the broader curriculum. The information and exercises that follow show children what they should be looking out for in any comprehension test, as well as strategies for improving their skills.

B Three steps to comprehension

Comprehension tasks will form a major part of all English tests you will take, from Year 1 SATs through to GCSE English. There are common problems in comprehension work that many children struggle with and under exam conditions these problems are often magnified. In timed tests, many capable pupils can easily lose precious marks.

If you can become more familiar with the skills required for comprehension exercises, it will help you to improve your performance in this type of test. This book will help you to develop the skills needed to sit a comprehension test confidently. It will show you:

- *how to find vital clues in the text*
- *how to recognise different text types*
- *what an examiner is looking for in the answers to a wide range of question types*
- *practical ways to check your work.*

This book is a practical guide to comprehension and is therefore packed with exercises and tasks that will help you to develop each skill. There is also a set of three test papers that combine all the skills you will have learned and will allow you to gain experience of sitting a test paper in mock exam conditions. Working through this book will help you to feel comfortable and confident with each of the skills you will need, ensuring you have the best possible grounding in comprehension.

1 Read and understand the text

● Find clues in the text

When completing any comprehension test there will be quite a lot of information to read and understand. As a result, holding all of these details, questions and ideas in your head can be difficult to do.

A valuable strategy to adopt when reading a text is to look for **keywords** and underline them as you read through the text for the first time. Keywords are those words and phrases that contain the most important information. They include:

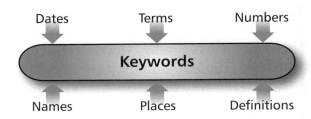

Another useful strategy is to **annotate** your text with handy tips or notes in the margin. These could relate to the keywords that you have found, your own active reading questions (we will look at these in the next section) or phrases that you don't understand. Here is an example of an annotated text:

Notes	Text
Could be written by a doctor? *Informative style* *Deficient?* *Modern and up to date* *Consume?* *Aim – to make us eat healthier* *Benefits of individual foods →*	It is so important to eat a <u>balanced diet</u> in order to keep our bodies healthy with all of the vitamins and minerals our bodies need to function correctly. If we do not eat a balanced diet, containing foods from the <u>five major food groups,</u> we could end up <u>deficient</u> in nutrients and this could have serious consequences. The <u>latest thinking</u> is that <u>fruit and vegetables</u> should play a major part in what we eat. Eating a variety of fruit and vegetables of <u>different colours</u> will ensure that we consume a range of nutrients. For example, <u>dark green vegetables</u> are rich in iron, whilst <u>purple and orange fruit and vegetables</u> are <u>high in vitamin C</u>. Bananas <u>contain beneficial potassium</u> and <u>onions are a powerful antiseptic</u> that can help to heal our bodies.

You can see here that several keywords are underlined in the text, making it easy to find the information again. There are also some brief notes in the margin that comment on:

- the possible identity of the author
- the style of writing
- the likely aim of the writing.

Any unknown terms have been drawn out in the margin with a question mark so they can be returned to later if necessary. Writing these types of notes while reading the text will help to make answering any set questions much more straightforward.

> ✓ **Parent Tip**
>
> *To help develop your child's skill in recognising keywords, encourage them to take notes as they read. Begin by reading a sentence together and asking them to pick out the keywords. Then try a couple of sentences and then a paragraph. If you pick an area of interest, such as the latest football match, a favourite programme or book, it will help to increase their interest in the task and turn it into a game. This way they should recognise which words are vital more quickly.*

● Discover active reading

Before you can answer any questions on a piece of comprehension, you must first make sure that you have understood what the text is about. This means that you need to **read actively**; to be aware of what you are reading. The best way to do this is to try and ask yourself a range of questions as you read. Thinking of as many as possible will put you in a strong position and some of them may directly answer several of the set questions.

Even if a set question does not seem completely related, reading actively will help you engage with the text more quickly and kick-start your analysis skills. For example, if a set question asks you to predict what could happen next, you should already be thinking about what is happening, where it is happening, why it is happening and what the aim of the text is. From the thoughts and ideas that your active reading will generate, you will be well on the way to answering many questions – saving you valuable time.

Remember that not all of these questions will be applicable for every comprehension extract and that you won't have long to make notes on them before you need to start answering the set questions. However, getting used to asking yourself a wide range of questions will provide you with a sound framework for approaching any type of text that is set.

Here are **ten key questions** to think about when reading a text for the first time:

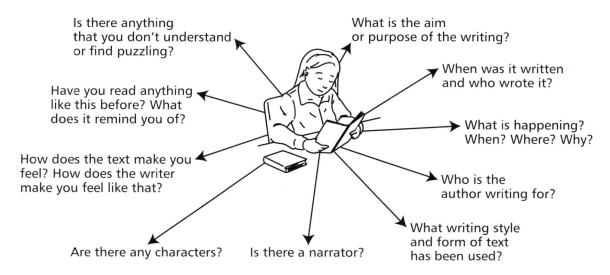

- Is there anything that you don't understand or find puzzling?
- Have you read anything like this before? What does it remind you of?
- How does the text make you feel? How does the writer make you feel like that?
- Are there any characters?
- Is there a narrator?
- What writing style and form of text has been used?
- Who is the author writing for?
- What is happening? When? Where? Why?
- When was it written and who wrote it?
- What is the aim or purpose of the writing?

Practise your skills of active reading with the following extract. Then look through each of the sections below to see if you found the right clues to answer the ten key questions as you read the text.

Remember to annotate the text by underlining the keywords and making notes in the margin. If you prefer to have the extract on a separate sheet of paper, follow the Free Resources link at www.bond11plus.co.uk and download a free copy.

> Once there were four children whose names were Peter, Susan, Edmund and Lucy. This story is about something that happened to them when they were sent away from London during the war because of the air-raids. They were sent to the house of an old Professor who lived in the heart of the country, ten miles from the nearest railway station and two miles from the nearest
> 5 post office. He had no wife and he lived in a very large house with a housekeeper called Mrs Macready and three servants. (Their names were Ivy, Margaret and Betty, but they do not come into the story much.) He himself was a very old man with shaggy white hair which grew over most of his face as well as on his head, and they liked him almost at once; but on the first evening when he came out to meet them at the front door he was so odd-looking
> 10 that Lucy (who was the youngest) was a little afraid of him, and Edmund (who was the next youngest) wanted to laugh and had to keep on pretending he was blowing his nose to hide it.
> As soon as they had said good night to the Professor and gone upstairs on the first night, the boys came into the girls' room and they all talked it over.
> "We've fallen on our feet and no mistake," said Peter. "This is going to be perfectly
> 15 splendid. That old chap will let us do anything we like."
> "I think he's an old dear," said Susan.
> "Oh, come off it!" said Edmund, who was tired and pretending not to be tired, which always made him bad-tempered. "Don't go on talking like that."
> "Like what?" said Susan; "and anyway, it's time you were in bed."
> 20 "Trying to talk like Mother," said Edmund. "And who are you to say when I'm to go to bed? Go to bed yourself."
> "Hadn't we all better go to bed?" said Lucy. "There's sure to be a row if we're heard talking here."
> "No there won't," said Peter. "I tell you this is the sort of house where no one's going
> 25 to mind what we do. Anyway, they won't hear us. It's about ten minutes' walk from here down to that dining-room, and any amount of stairs and passages in between."
> "What's that noise?" said Lucy suddenly. It was a far larger house than she had ever been in before and the thought of all those long passages and rows of doors leading into empty rooms was beginning to make her feel a little creepy.

"It's only a bird, silly," said Edmund.

"It's an owl," said Peter. "This is going to be a wonderful place for birds. I shall go to bed now. I say, let's go and explore tomorrow. You might find anything in a place like this. Did you see those mountains as we came along? And the woods? There might be eagles. There might be stags. There'll be hawks."

"Badgers!" said Lucy.

"Foxes!" said Edmund.

"Rabbits!" said Susan.

But when next morning came there was a steady rain falling, so thick that when you looked out of the window you could see neither the mountains nor the woods nor even the stream in the garden.

"Of course it *would* be raining!" said Edmund.

They had just finished their breakfast with the Professor and were upstairs in the room he had set apart for them – a long, low room with two windows looking out in one direction and two in another.

"Do stop grumbling, Ed," said Susan. "Ten to one it'll clear up in an hour or so. And in the meantime we're pretty well off. There's a wireless and lots of books."

"Not for me," said Peter; "I'm going to explore in the house."

Everyone agreed to this and that was how the adventures began. It was the sort of house that you never seem to come to the end of, and it was full of unexpected places. The first few doors they tried led only into spare bedrooms, as everyone had expected that they would; but soon they came to a very long room full of pictures and there they found a suit of armour; and after that was a room all hung with green, with a harp in one corner; and then came three steps down and five steps up, and then a kind of little upstairs hall and a door that led out on to a balcony, and then a whole series of rooms that led into each other and were lined with books – most of them very old books and some bigger than a Bible in a church. And shortly after that they looked into a room that was quite empty except for one big wardrobe; the sort that has a looking-glass in the door. There was nothing else in the room at all except a dead bluebottle on the window sill.

"Nothing there!" said Peter, and they all trooped out again – all except Lucy. She stayed behind because she thought it would be worth while trying the door of the wardrobe, even though she felt almost sure that it would be locked. To her surprise it opened quite easily, and two moth-balls dropped out.

Looking into the inside, she saw several coats hanging up – mostly long fur coats. There was nothing Lucy liked so much as the smell and feel of fur. She immediately stepped into the wardrobe and got in among the coats and rubbed her face against them, leaving the door open, of course, because she knew that it is very foolish to shut oneself into any wardrobe. Soon she went further in and found that there was a second row of coats hanging up behind the first one. It was almost quite dark in there and she kept her arms stretched out in front of her so as not to bump her face into the back of the wardrobe. She took a step further in – then two or three steps – always expecting to feel woodwork against the tips of her fingers. But she could not feel it.

"This must be a simply enormous wardrobe!" thought Lucy, going still further in and pushing the soft folds of the coats aside to make room for her. Then she noticed that there was something crunching under her feet. "I wonder is that more moth-balls?" she thought, stooping down to feel it with her hand. But instead of feeling the hard, smooth wood of the floor of the wardrobe, she felt something soft and powdery and extremely cold. "This is very queer," she said, and went on a step or two further.

Next moment she found that what was rubbing against her face and hands was no longer soft fur but something hard and rough and even prickly. "Why, it is just like branches of trees!" exclaimed Lucy. And then she saw that there was a light ahead of her; not a few inches away where the back of the wardrobe ought to have been, but a long way off. Something cold and soft was falling on her. A moment later she found that she was standing in the middle of a wood at night-time with snow under her feet and snowflakes falling through the air.

From *The Lion, the Witch and the Wardrobe* by C. S. Lewis

How did you do? How many questions did you think about as you read through the passage? Did you start to feel like a detective searching for clues?

Now let's have a closer look at the range of questions and see how answering them as you read can help to improve your understanding of a comprehension text.

a) What is the aim or purpose of the writing?

Which keywords did you find that indicated the aim or the purpose of this text? Did you spot these vital clues?

All of this evidence leads us to the conclusion that this extract has been taken from a children's story and that its aim must be to draw the reader into an exciting tale of adventure.

Being able to work out the aim and purpose straight away will give you a good head start in many comprehension exams.

> **Skills checklist**
>
> *Thinking about the purpose of a piece of writing can help you to:*
>
> ☐ understand the meaning of a text
> ☐ understand and interpret key pieces of information
> ☐ recognise a writer's aim and viewpoint
> ☐ show your word knowledge.

b) When was it written and who wrote it?

Which keywords indicate when this text was written and who wrote it? Did you spot that the children were sent to the country during the war (lines 2–4)?

Which wars can you think of that involved air raids over London? The Second World War is the most recent, so the story is likely to be set during 1939–1945, but you would not be expected to know the exact dates. If you knew that it was set in wartime or even that it was in the 1940s, it would help you to place the extract in a historical setting. This is important because many features of language have changed since this time. Children do not commonly use phrases like 'old chap' (line 15), 'perfectly splendid' (lines 14–15) and 'looking-glass' (line 57) today.

Did you notice that the author's name followed the title? Have you heard of this author before? Can you think of any other books written by the same author? Knowing about other books an author has written could be useful when trying to work out what type of book an extract has come from, who it is aimed at and what might happen next.

> **Skills checklist**
>
> *Finding clues about when a text was written and who wrote it can help you to:*
> - ☐ understand and interpret key pieces of information
> - ☐ place a text into a historical context
> - ☐ explain a writer's use of language, grammar and literary features.

c) What is happening? When? Where? Why?

Which keywords explain **what** is happening? There were plenty of clues in this extract relating to the plot of this story. You should have grasped the following key points from reading the text:

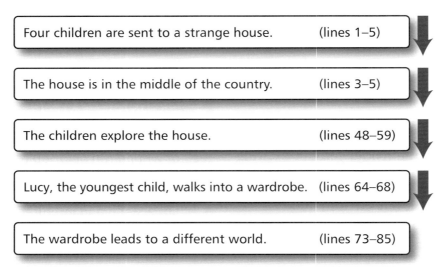

Understanding these basic events is crucial not only for making sense of what is going on, but also for predicting what might follow. You are left thinking: Where is Lucy? Will the other children find her? Will Lucy be safe? What will Lucy see in the woods and why is it snowing?

Which keywords explain **when** the events are happening? We have already thought about the historical reference to the war, relating to when the text was written. Now we need to look for more specific detail to find out when these events are happening in the story.

We are told that:

- *this is the first full day that the children have been in the house (lines 12–13 and 38)*
- *Lucy finds the wardrobe after a number of other rooms have been explored (lines 50–62).*

Looking at the sequence of events more closely is important because it will help you to understand what is happening, as well as to put the chain of events in order.

Which keywords explain **where** the events are happening? Again, we know generally where the children are (in an old house in the countryside) but now we must consider the finer details to find out where the events occur.

The secrets of Comprehension

We are given:

- a detailed account of the house with its many rooms and passages (lines 25–29; 48–58)
- a lengthy description of Lucy as she opens the wardrobe and moves through the fur coats into the forest (lines 60–85).

We need to understand where the action of a story is placed because this could be very important for the plot later on. For example, in this part of the story we read about many different rooms and find out that the room with the wardrobe leads to another world. Does this mean that all the rooms will lead to different worlds? Maybe the room with the harp and the room with the suit of armour will lead to other adventures. Will the children and the reader need to remember which room leads to the forest as the story continues?

Which keywords explain **why** the events are happening? 'Why' is an important question to ask regularly as you read through a text. It can form the basis for many different questions; questions which often require a personal response.

Here are some examples that may have come to mind while reading the extract:

Why has this extract been given?

Why did Edmund pretend not to be tired?

Why were the children sent to the country?

Why did Lucy think she was walking on mothballs?

If you thought about the first question, you might consider that:

- line 1 indicates this is the opening scene of a story
- the extract sets the scene for us:
  - It introduces the main characters (lines 1; 10–11; 14–37; 45–47).
  - It provides an explanation of why they are at the house (lines 2–3).
  - It describes how Lucy finds herself in the woods (lines 47–49; 64 onwards).
  - It leaves us to guess what might happen next.

▶ Skills checklist

Asking yourself what, when, where and why something is happening can help you to answer questions that require you to:

- ☐ understand the meaning of a text
- ☐ understand and interpret key pieces of information
- ☐ recognise a writer's aim and viewpoint
- ☐ comment on the structure, order and presentation of a text
- ☐ summarise part of a text
- ☐ explain a writer's use of language, grammar and literary features
- ☐ continue a piece of writing
- ☐ give your opinion on a text
- ☐ use clues from the text to predict what will happen next.

d) Who is the author writing for?

Were there any keywords that implied who the target reader might be? Here are some key details that should help you deduce who this text has been written for:

From these points it seems logical to conclude that this story has been written for older children who are able readers.

It is also a good idea to think about the scenarios described in a text, as these can be a useful clue to the likely readership. For example:

- *Have you ever felt a little afraid when meeting someone new, like Lucy?*
- *Have you sneaked out of bed at night and been worried about getting caught?*
- *Do you get grumpy when you are over-tired?*
- *Have you ever been scared by night-time noises?*

These aren't experiences or reactions that an adult is likely to have, but children will definitely be able to understand and relate to these events.

> ### Skills checklist
>
> *Developing a sense of the target audience will help you to:*
>
> - [ ] understand the meaning of a text
> - [ ] understand and interpret key pieces of information
> - [ ] recognise a writer's aim and viewpoint
> - [ ] place a text into a historical context.

e) What writing style and form of text has been used?

In order to fully understand a piece of writing you must first be able to decode the text. This means you need to find the descriptors (the clues) that will help you decide what type of text it is and the writing style it uses. We can work out the style by looking at physical features, vocabulary and purpose. These are some typical physical features found in different styles:

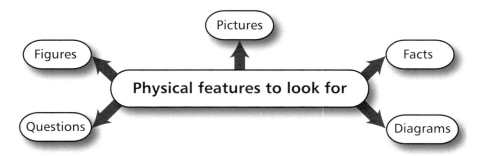

Here are some key questions to ask about the type of vocabulary:

- *Do the words mainly show positive or negative traits?*
- *Is there an emphasis on description, facts, emotion or humour?*
- *Is the author trying to persuade the reader to laugh, cry, empathise or understand a viewpoint?*
- *Does the writing use Standard English or colloquial, everyday speech?*

You can clarify the purpose of the writing by asking questions such as:

- *Does the writing entertain the reader?*
- *Does the writing inform the reader?*
- *Does the writing instruct or guide the reader?*

What clues did you find in the extract that told you about the writing style and form of this text?

- *This is continuous text arranged in paragraphs.*
- *It is full of description and detail.*
- *There are no bulleted lists, diagrams or subheadings.*

} This is a piece of prose.

- *Speech is integrated within the text, not written on separate lines following each character's name.*

} More likely to be from a novel than a playscript.

- *This is a children's story.*
- *Uses phrases such as: 'that was how the adventures began'.*

} The writer aims to entertain the reader.

How did you do? Did you spot all these clues? Understanding the writing style and form of a text is a vital skill in comprehension because many typical questions can be based on these elements. We will look at these aspects in more detail in the 'Recognise different text types' section later (pages 27–38).

▶ Skills checklist

Working out the writing style and format of a text can help you to:

- ☐ understand and interpret key pieces of information
- ☐ recognise the overall effects a text has on the reader
- ☐ select, describe or find information from the text
- ☐ comment on the structure, order and presentation of a text
- ☐ explain a writer's use of language, grammar and literary features
- ☐ show your word knowledge and spelling skills
- ☐ show your understanding of vocabulary within context
- ☐ show your knowledge of sentence structure and order
- ☐ support your comments by referring to, or quoting from, the text.

f) Is there a narrator?

The narrator is the storyteller. Which words in the text imply the identity of the narrator?

Often the author is the narrator, but not always. Sometimes:

- we tell our own story ⟶ The **first person** narrative

  'There was nothing **I** liked so much as the smell and feel of fur.'

- the narrator refers directly to you, the reader ⟶ The **second person** narrative

  'There was nothing **you** liked so much as the smell and feel of fur.'

- a story is told through the eye of an observer ⟶ The **third person** narrative

  'There was nothing **Lucy** liked so much as the smell and feel of fur.'

It is important to work out the identity of the narrator straight away because this can determine how we read something. Looking out for characters' names or references to 'I' will help you to distinguish who is narrating a text.

> **Top Tip**
> The second person narrative is the least common form of writing.

Here are some key points to note about each narrative form:

- *1st person narrative*
  You may often assume the writing is more factual and true as the narrator refers to his or her own feelings and thoughts. However, remember that you are only hearing about events from one point of view and the text could therefore be biased.
- *2nd person narrative*
  A story or account written in this form involves the reader in the events being described. It talks directly to the audience and takes them along on the journey.
- *3rd person narrative*
  This often gives a more objective overview of what is happening. It allows all characters' voices and opinions to be heard and gives more background and detail to events than a first-person narrator could provide.

Did you detect the narrator in this extract? The pronouns 'he', 'she' and 'they' as well as characters' names are used frequently in this text. Look at the quote below. The characters' names and pronouns are highlighted in bold.

> "What's that noise?" said **Lucy** suddenly. It was a far larger house than **she** had ever been in before and the thought of all those long passages and rows of doors leading into empty rooms was beginning to make **her** feel a little creepy.
> "It's only a bird, silly," said **Edmund**.

We also hear the thoughts and opinions of many different characters in this text so the narrator cannot be one of the characters. Here is an example using the same quote:

> "What's that noise?" said Lucy suddenly. **It was a far larger house than she had ever been in before and the thought of all those long passages and rows of doors leading into empty rooms was beginning to make her feel a little creepy.**
> "It's only a bird, silly," said Edmund.

How can the narrator know how Lucy feels? The narrator must be either the author or an outside observer, so it is clear that this text is written in the third person.

▶ Skills checklist

Discovering the identity of the narrator can help you to:
- [ ] understand the meaning of a text
- [ ] understand and interpret key pieces of information
- [ ] recognise the overall effects the text has on the reader
- [ ] place a text within a historical context
- [ ] understand, describe or select information from a text
- [ ] comment on the structure, order and presentation of a text
- [ ] explain a writer's use of language, grammar and literary features
- [ ] continue a piece of writing
- [ ] give your interpretation or opinion of a text
- [ ] use clues from the text to predict what will happen next.

g) Are there any characters?

What did the extract tell you about the characters? Think about how the author has started to develop each character. Which keywords are used to describe their appearance and actions or give clues about their personality?

Let's look at what we can learn about the Professor from lines 3–6 in the first paragraph:

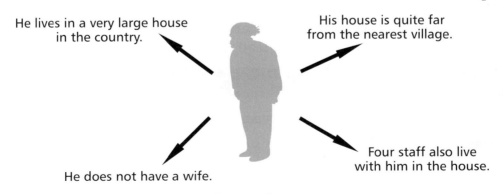

The Professor

What can we deduce from these facts? Perhaps he is lonely and will enjoy having the children to stay. Or he may prefer his privacy and so not really want the children in his home. Are we given any other information that might support one of these ideas?

How did the children react when they first met him? We are told that they liked him straight away (line 8), so this implies the Professor has a kindly nature and is happy to let the children stay with him.

We can also start to build a picture of what he looks like. Lines 7–8 tell us that:

- *he is a very old man*
- *he has messy white hair*
- *he has a shaggy white beard.*

From the description of Lucy and Edmund's reactions when they first meet him (lines 9–11), we can also conclude that the Professor must look a bit strange!

What about Lucy? What does the text tell us about her character?

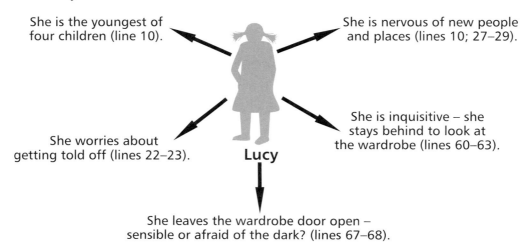

Can you see how you can use the information in a text to develop pictures of characters? Did you pick up on all of these clues about the Professor and Lucy as you read the extract?

Comprehension questions often ask about a character's personality, actions or possible motivations so, when characters are introduced, it is important to try and build up a picture of them. The more you know about the characters, the easier it should be to predict how and why they might behave in a particular way. Take care to note down as many clues as you can while you read.

Top Tip

It can be helpful to draw quick flow charts or 'spider' diagrams like the ones shown for the Professor and Lucy when making notes about characters.

Skills checklist

Building up a picture of a character's appearance, personality and actions can help you to:

- [ ] understand the meaning of a text
- [ ] understand and interpret key pieces of information
- [ ] recognise a writer's aim and viewpoint
- [ ] summarise part of a text
- [ ] recognise the overall effects the text has on the reader
- [ ] understand, describe or select information from a text

> **Skills checklist** *continued*
> - ☐ explain a writer's use of language, grammar and literary features
> - ☐ give your interpretation or opinion of a text
> - ☐ use clues from the text to predict what will happen next
> - ☐ support your comments by referring to, or quoting from, the text.

(h) How does the text make you feel? How does the writer make you feel like that?

Can you describe how you felt when you were reading the extract? Which words or phrases do you think helped to make you feel like that?

We are told that this is going to be an adventure story (line 48). How does this type of story usually make you feel?

Let's look more closely at the words and phrases the author uses; these will hold the clues to the author's technique.

In the first 47 lines of the extract, the author provides us with quite a lot of background detail. We are given:

- the reason why the children are in the country
- a description of the owner of the house
- some hints as to the personality of each child.

All of this information helps set the scene for us, so that we can really imagine where the children are and start to get to know them. There is very little action in these opening scenes – that is to come from line 48 onwards.

Here is the next section of text again:

> It was the sort of house that you never seem to come to the end of, and it was full of unexpected places. The first few doors they tried led only into spare bedrooms, as everyone had expected that they would; but soon they came to a very long room full of pictures and there they found a suit of armour; and after that was a room all hung with green, with a
> 5 harp in one corner; and then came three steps down and five steps up, and then a kind of little upstairs hall and a door that led out on to a balcony, and then a whole series of rooms that led into each other and were lined with books – most of them very old books and some bigger than a Bible in a church. And shortly after that they looked into a room that was quite empty except for one big wardrobe; the sort that has a looking-glass in the
> 10 door. There was nothing else in the room at all except a dead bluebottle on the window sill.

What do you notice? The author gradually builds a picture of the children's discoveries by writing about them, one after the other, in the same sentence (lines 2–8) above. We follow them from room to room, questioning what they see and not knowing what they are going to find next.

Will they stumble across a forgotten treasure chest?
Will they find a body?
Is there someone in the suit of armour?
Why is one room all decorated in green?
Who does the harp belong to?
Who are the pictures of?
Who reads all of these books?

As we think about these types of questions, the tension we feel starts to rise, and it increases when Lucy is separated from the others. We know that she is the youngest child; will she be all right on her own? Now we are getting nervous. What will happen when she opens the wardrobe door? What will she find? A ghost? No, we can relax. She finds nothing more than some old coats!

But then Lucy steps into the wardrobe, keeps her arms outstretched and touches… nothing. The tension is mounting again.

Where is she going?
Why isn't there a back to the wardrobe?
What will she find in the dark?

With phrases such as 'she took a step further in – then two or three steps …' the author steadily builds our anticipation for what is coming next.

At the same time our **senses** are stirring. It is dark so Lucy cannot *see* but she can *smell* and *feel* the fur coats. She *hears* something crunching under her feet; she bends down to *touch* it and *feels* something soft and cold. By using the senses of the character, the author also heightens our response to the story.

As a reader we have to imagine what is going on, and a successful author will help us to see, hear, feel, smell, taste and touch in the same way as the character. Using words and phrases that appeal to our senses helps a story to come alive in our imagination, and this is how an author makes a reader feel different emotions. The better we know a character, the stronger our emotional attachment to them will become and the stronger our reaction to the resolution or climax of the story is likely to be.

Did you feel tense, nervous and excited as you read through the extract? Were you able to imagine how the fur coats would feel? Could you hear Lucy's footsteps crunching on the ground?

▶ Skills checklist

Being able to describe how a text makes you feel, and working out the techniques an author has used to make you feel like that, can help you to:

- ☐ understand the meaning of a text
- ☐ understand and interpret key pieces of information
- ☐ recognise a writer's aim and viewpoint

> ### Skills checklist continued

- [ ] recognise the overall effects the text has on the reader
- [ ] explain a writer's use of language, grammar and literary features
- [ ] select, describe or find information from the text
- [ ] show your word knowledge and spelling skills
- [ ] give your opinion on a text.

(i) Have you read anything like this before? What does it remind you of?

This is an important question to think about as you read through a comprehension text. Thinking about an extract in relation to something that you have read before can help you to understand what is happening.

You may already have answered this question when thinking about who the author is and what else they have written. If not, ask yourself whether you have read or watched anything that had a similar plot, or used similar language or was perhaps set in the same time period. The text may have reminded you of a film or television programme that you have watched. Maybe it reminds you of something personal that you have experienced yourself.

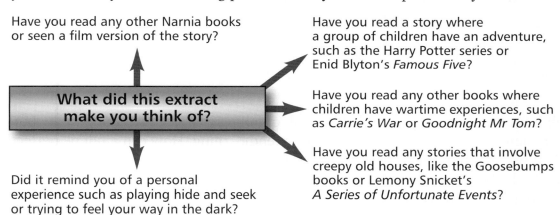

> ### Skills checklist

Thinking about what a text reminds you of can make it easier to:

- [ ] understand the meaning of a text
- [ ] understand key pieces of information
- [ ] recognise the overall effects the text has on the reader
- [ ] summarise part of the text
- [ ] show your word knowledge and spelling skills
- [ ] give your opinion on a text
- [ ] use clues from the text to predict what will happen next
- [ ] support your comments by quoting from, or referring to, the text.

j) Is there anything that you don't understand or find puzzling?

Were there any words or phrases you didn't understand as you read through the extract? Did you make a note of them in the margin so you could try to work them out later?

When you read a piece of writing it may include several unfamiliar words that are difficult to understand. This is especially true when a text is written in dialect, uses slang words or includes subject-specific language.

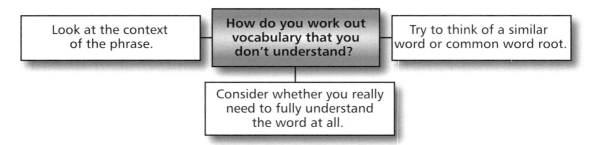

Here are three examples of words or phrases from the extract that you may not have been familiar with. One of the above strategies is used to work out what each one means.

- *'fallen on our feet'* (line 14)

With an unfamiliar phrase like this, you need to think about it in relation to the sentences before and after it. This will help you to understand the context, which will give clues to the meaning. So let's look at this in full.

> "We've fallen on our feet and no mistake," said Peter. "This is going to be perfectly splendid. That old chap will let us do anything we like."

If you fall it is often painful; you probably think of falling as a negative thing to do, but the context here suggests that it is a 'perfectly splendid' thing. How can a fall be perfectly splendid? If we fall on our feet, have we really fallen at all? Maybe it means that if we are going to fall, the best way to land is on our feet, making it more of a 'trip' than actually falling down and injuring ourselves. Perhaps what Peter is saying, then, is that being away from their parents may be a horrible situation to be in, but it could be a lot worse. Staying in this old house could turn out to be a good experience because the old Professor is kind and will let them do whatever they want.

- *'looking-glass'* (line 57)

We can see this as two words, 'looking' and 'glass', but does this help us understand the term any better? What other words can mean 'looking'?

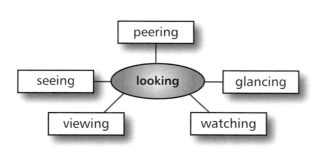

If we put these words alongside 'glass' we get:

seeing glass (like glasses?)

peering glass

glancing glass

watching glass (like a mirror?)

viewing glass (like a microscope?).

Would glasses, microscope or mirror make sense in the sentence?

'one big wardrobe; the sort that has $\begin{Bmatrix} \text{glasses} \\ \text{a mirror} \\ \text{a microscope} \end{Bmatrix}$ in the door.'

The only sensible answer here is a mirror, because some wardrobes do have a mirror in the door.

- 'stags' (line 34)

If you don't know what a stag is and you can't work out the full meaning from the context or think of any similar words or any that share the same word root, perhaps it is not a vital word to understand. Let's have a look at the section this word is in.

> "You might find anything in a place like this. Did you see those mountains as we came along? And the woods? There might be eagles. There might be stags. There'll be hawks."
> "Badgers!" said Lucy.
> "Foxes!" said Edmund.
> "Rabbits!" said Susan.

From reading the surrounding text it seems that a stag is some kind of wild animal or bird that lives in the mountains or woods. Why has the term been included here? Do you think it will be vital to the plot? What does this section of speech tell us about the children?

It is likely that the author has included stags in this section to help highlight the fact that the children are now in the middle of the countryside. Listing different birds and animals shows that their new environment is likely to hold many surprises. For city children, this is going to be a place where they can explore and get close to animals they would not normally see. The term 'stag' is therefore not overly important on its own.

▶ Skills checklist

It is useful to identify any terms that you find puzzling as you read through a text. Some of them may be used in some of the set questions, so if you have already started thinking about them it will help you to:

- ☐ understand the meaning of a text
- ☐ understand key pieces of information
- ☐ summarise part of the text
- ☐ explain a writer's use of language, grammar and literary features
- ☐ show your word knowledge and spelling skills
- ☐ show your understanding of vocabulary within context
- ☐ show your knowledge of sentence structure and order.

Now it's your turn!

Now that we have worked through the ten key active reading questions in detail, let's look at how they might relate to some set questions that could accompany this comprehension text. Reread the extract on pages 9–10 and answer the questions below. Notice how many you will have already answered or started to think about through following an active reading approach.

1 Join each child to the correct animal.

Lucy   rabbits

Edmund   badgers

Susan   stags

Peter   foxes

☐ 4

2 Underline the child who states that there is a wireless and lots of books.

Lucy   Edmund   Susan   Peter

☐ 1

3 Underline the two statements that are true.

   a There was a green room full of pictures.   **b** There was a suit of armour in one room.

   c There was a harp in a very long room.   **d** One door led onto a balcony.

   e The little upstairs hall had a very old book in it.

☐ 2

4 Underline the two statements that are false.

   a Mrs Macready was the Professor's wife.   **b** There was a servant called Ivy.

   c The post office was ten miles away from the house.   **d** The Professor was a very old man.

   e The Professor lived in the heart of the country.

☐ 2

5 Explain in your own words why the country was safer than London.

_____
_____
_____
_____

☐ 2

6 Why was Lucy afraid of the Professor? Refer to the text in your answer.

_____
_____
_____

☐ 2

7 Write a definition for the following words as used in the text:

a splendid (line 15) _____

_____

b trooped (line 60) _____

_____ [2]

8 How would you describe Edmund? Refer to the text in your answer.

_____
_____
_____
_____
_____ [5]

9 How do you feel at the end of this extract and why?

_____
_____
_____
_____
_____
_____ [5]

10 Why do you think the author chooses Lucy to walk into the wardrobe? Explain your opinion.

_____
_____
_____
_____
_____
_____
_____
_____ [5]

[30 TOTAL]

END OF TEST

How many of these questions were quite easy to answer after reading actively? Turn to page 104 to work out your score.

The table below shows which active reading questions should have been useful in answering the questions above. If you have lost marks in any question, go back to the appropriate section and reread it to make sure you understand what to look out for when reading actively.

Question number / Active reading question	a	b	c	d	e	f	g	h	i	j
1							✓			
2							✓			
3			✓							
4			✓				✓			
5		✓								
6							✓			
7					✓				✓	✓
8			✓	✓			✓			
9					✓	✓		✓		
10	✓		✓	✓			✓		✓	

 Top Tip

Remember that what is not said in a text can be as important as what is said. This forms the basis of 'reading between the lines'.

 Active reading can be like a tangled ball of string with each knotted strand attached to a balloon. When you have untangled which strand belongs to which balloon, you are left with many neat strands so that you can select any of the balloons at any time with the least amount of difficulty. Each balloon represents one of these key questions and the strand of each balloon weaves its way through the text.

 Top Tip

You really do have to be a detective sometimes to uncover every possible clue that can give you the evidence you need. In order to get the most out of any reading: THINK, QUESTION, and RESPOND. This will help you to be as well-prepared as possible for the examiner's questions.

Now that we have thought about how to read actively, let's have a look at how to recognise different types of text.

● Recognise different text types

It is important to be able to recognise the type of source an extract has been taken from because it can provide valuable clues to the aim or purpose of the writing and the audience it has been written for. It can also help you to predict what might happen next, to highlight literary features and writing techniques, and can be useful when writing a continuation of a text. Let's have a look at a range of sources that comprehension extracts may be taken from.

a) *Narrative texts*

Narrative texts, such as stories or fictional prose, usually consist of continuous text set out in paragraphs, with the whole storyline, or plot, divided into sections called chapters. They usually follow a structure that has a beginning, middle and end, but events in narrative texts do not have to be written in chronological order.

Certain forms of narrative text have their own recognisable features. For example, traditional fairy stories often begin with the phrase, 'Once upon a time…'. Science fiction (Sci Fi) narratives often include a range of invented words, such as 'Cephalochromoscope' or new collocations (combinations of words), such as 'Causality Violation Device Probe'. These made-up terms help to make a text sound more futuristic.

The aim of narrative texts is to entertain, and to do this the writing style often includes a mixture of techniques, such as description, persuasion, literal writing and figurative imagery. A range of themes, such as humour, suspense and action are also commonly found in this style of writing.

> **Key Facts**
>
> Narrative texts:
> - consist of continuous text written in paragraphs
> - have a clear structure: beginning, middle, end
> - entertain the reader using a variety of writing styles and themes
> - can be character based, where the text concentrates on the experience of a character
> - can be plot based, where the setting and storylines are the most important elements
> - have a narrator; this role can be taken either by one or more characters, or by the writer
> - can be written in the first, second or third person
> - can include dialogue, shown as direct or reported speech.

Let's have a look at two examples of narrative text.

> **A** The navigational computer unit whirred into action compensating for the gravitational influence of the sonar tripod. Was it possible for the spaceship to travel through the dark matter without being sucked into oblivion? Only the deathstar stood between them and the unknown. The captain consulted the astrogation monitor before hitting the red button...
>
> **B** It was yesterday when I first noticed the box that was on the next door neighbour's doorstep. It was large, blue and shimmered in the sun. "Is it Mr Mundy's birthday?" I asked dad as he unlocked the car. "I don't know!" he replied. "Why on earth do you ask that?" I could see he was in a rush so I just shrugged and climbed into the back of the car. I forgot all about it until I returned home from school and saw that the box was still there.

Now it's your turn!

Can you find six typical features of narrative texts in extracts A and B? The first one has been done for you.

1 *There are characters in both texts: 'the captain' in A and 'I', 'dad' and 'Mr Mundy' in B.*
2 _____
3 _____
4 _____
5 _____
6 _____

b) Poetry

Poems can be written in one, undivided column of text or can be written in stanzas (verses). Lines of poetry are shorter than prose because they are not written in continuous text. Lines may have a clear rhyming pattern, and usually each new line starts with a capital letter.

Different types of poetry (or verse) have their own recognisable features. For example, a sonnet is traditionally a love poem consisting of 14 lines, whereas a limerick is a humorous poem that has only five lines and follows a distinctive rhythm. Poems are written in many styles and they can cover a wide range of themes, such as humour, emotion, recounts, songs and riddles.

  Key Facts

Poems:
- can be written in a straight column of text or in stanzas
- usually have a clear rhythm
- use fewer words and fewer, shorter lines than prose

The secrets of Comprehension

> **Key Facts** *continued*
>
> - often start each new line with a capital letter
> - generally follow rhyming patterns but don't have to rhyme
> - use punctuation to create rhythmic effects such as allowing lines to run on (enjambment) or creating pauses in the middle of lines (caesura)
> - contain a range of sound effects (such as alliteration, onomatopoeia, elisions – ne'er, e'er and so on)
> - regularly include literary effects such as imagery (simile, metaphor)
> - may introduce archaic language (such as 'doth' for 'does')
> - can cover a wide range of themes.

Let's have a look at two examples of poetry.

A
For Thine is the Kingdom
All creation kneel in wonder.
From birds and beasts in sea and air,
To sunshine, rain and thunder.
For eternal days, may all sing praise:
"Creation to Creator,
Let ne'er be put asunder."

Let creation praise Thee

B
There was a young lad from Crewe,
Who wasn't sure how he would do.
But he did try his best
In his 11+ test,
And now he waits for the results to come through!

The 11+ limerick

Now it's your turn!

Can you find six typical features of poetic texts in extracts A and B? The first one has been done for you.

1. *Each new line in both poems starts with a capital letter.*
2. _____
3. _____
4. _____
5. _____
6. _____

c) Scripts

Scripts are plays written for the stage, radio, television or film so actors can act out a storyline or plot. They look noticeably different from other forms of text because they consist mostly of dialogue. The plot and development of each character is therefore seen largely through speech and direct action. Notes on the characters' actions and movements, setting, props, lighting and music are known as stage directions and are written in brackets within the text.

Particular forms of script have their own recognisable features. A monologue, for example, is a script that only has one character, whereas a farce has lots of characters rushing on and off the stage in a fast-paced, funny performance. There are many styles and themes that can be represented in script form, but tragedy, suspense, comedy, romance, religious or historical re-enactment and real-life events are most common.

 Key Facts

Scripts:
- divide the plot into acts and each act is divided into scenes
- mainly consist of dialogue, which can be written phonetically to give an authentic feel
- list the names of characters on the left-hand side of the page
- use a colon to separate a character's name from their dialogue
- start a new line when a different character speaks
- do not use speech marks
- show stage directions in brackets
- can include a narrator to link between scenes or to draw attention to the drama
- are based on a wide range of themes.

Let's have a look at two examples of scripts.

A **Act II, Scene 1: One week after the move**

[Lights come up to find Joyce and Bob in master bedroom; Joyce with paintbrush in hand, both in overalls.]

JOYCE: But I am sick of it all. The paint, the dust, the mess, it's so… *[Flops into a chair.]*

BOB: I know, but we're getting there. *[Puts his hand gently on her shoulder.]*

[Doorbell rings and the sound of feet is heard coming upstairs. Jon enters.]

JON: Mum, Dad… there are two men downstairs and they look really important!

B NARRATOR: It was a dark, cold night when Sam came out of the office. He'd had a really rough day and didn't want to think about work as he trudged home. Suddenly, from the shadows, a voice calls out…

JOE: Hey Sam! What's with the stayin' late?

[Sam stops and looks over towards the figure which is now under a street lamp.]

SAM: Alright Joe! *[looks at watch]* Gee, it's later than I thought. You still outta work?

JOE: Erm, well, yeah but I gotta interview next Wednesday…

Now it's your turn!

Can you find six typical features of scripted texts in extracts A and B? The first one has been done for you.

1. *Both extracts list the characters' names on the left and separate them from the dialogue with a colon.*
2. ___
3. ___
4. ___
5. ___
6. ___

d) Explanatory texts

Explanatory texts, such as textbooks, web sites or leaflets, are usually written in continuous text that is arranged in paragraphs and follows a clear structure. Content is often accompanied by graphic representations such as diagrams, charts, bulleted lists or maps, as these can help explain key concepts or facts to the reader. The purpose of explanatory texts is to inform and explain and to show a cause and effect. As there is such a diverse range of topics and themes that can be covered, the layout and writing styles of explanatory texts are extremely varied.

Certain forms of explanatory text have their own recognisable features. For example, a dictionary entry explains individual words and has their definition, language origination, pronunciation and examples of the word usage. A web site explanatory text may offer cross-reference links that open up a new window to explain connected topics or a pop-up glossary box relating to a highlighted keyword.

Key Facts

Explanatory texts:
- explain a topic clearly to the reader
- are written in continuous text
- are well structured: introduction, main content arranged in paragraphs, conclusion
- are written in an objective, formal style that shows no bias
- often include technical, subject-specific language
- usually include navigational aids (such as headings, footnotes and cross-reference links)
- highlight keywords clearly
- often use connective words to show cause and effect (such as 'so' or 'because')
- frequently include diagrams, charts, tables, lists, and so on.

Let's have a look at an example of an explanatory text.

Who is the author writing for?

How many keywords did you find? Here are some points that should help you:

As a result, it seems logical to conclude that the story has been written for older children who are able readers. The **scenarios** described in a text can also be a useful clue to the readership.

For example:

- Have you sneaked out of bed at night?
- Have you ever been scared by night-time noises?

These aren't experiences adults are likely to have, but children will definitely relate to them.

(*For more details on this topic, see Section 4.*)

Now it's your turn!

Can you find six typical features of explanatory texts in this extract? The first one has been done for you.

1 *The text includes a diagram.*
2 _____
3 _____
4 _____
5 _____
6 _____

e) Recounts and reports

Recounts and reports, such as magazine or newspaper articles, historical events, interviews, diary entries and biographies, share many features. They can be fictional or non-fictional, but are usually written in continuous text, following an organised structure. They often include diagrams, graphs, charts or pictures and can focus on many topics or themes.

Key Facts

Recounts **and** reports:
- retell a broad range of events or experiences
- can be factual or fictional
- follow a clear structure: introduction, main section in paragraphs, conclusion
- use navigational aids (such as headings and captions)
- introduce subject-specific or technical language if needed
- may include external quotes
- often include graphic features (such as graphs, diagrams, maps, illustrations and cartoons)
- are usually written in a formal style.

They also have their own individual characteristics. A recount is used to describe events, usually in chronological order. It is written in the past tense and uses connectives that signal time, such as 'first', 'then', 'next' and 'finally'. A recount focuses on facts and details using specific names and places.

 Key Facts

Recounts:
- are usually written in chronological order
- are written in the past tense
- include time connectives
- focus on specific facts
- are written in the first person.

A report is used to relate facts and is often non-chronological. It is written in the present tense in the third person narrative. The sentences are often passive and can include technical language. It talks in more general terms, rather than mentioning specific names, places or individual people.

 Key Facts

Reports:
- are often written in non-chronological order
- are written in the present tense
- contain mainly passive sentences
- focus on general points
- are written in the third person.

Let's have a look at two examples of recounts and reports.

A   WHAT HAVE THE ROMANS EVER DONE FOR US?

Has modern society really benefited from the legacy left by the Romans?

Modern services

The Romans had a huge influence on 21st century life. It is possible to trace the origins of many of today's services back to Roman times. Without them, transport, communication and sanitation systems might not have been as advanced or widespread as they are now. Even modern luxuries, such as central heating, have evolved from the Romans.

Language

The Romans brought the skills of reading and writing to Britain. Before they arrived, stories and traditions were passed on to each generation by word of mouth. They changed this by showing British people how to write. The Romans spoke and wrote in Latin, and many modern English terms have their roots in this ancient language.

B

The Railway Inn, Holly Hall

"Good value, great atmosphere, excellent service!"

A Gastronomic Delight!

My first visit to The Railway Inn; certainly not my last.

We arrived at 7 p.m. on Friday, without booking a table. A painless 20-minute wait presented us with a cosy table in the corner.

Our first taste of the menu was the home-made soup of the day, which was delicious. Then the organic vegetable casserole followed, served with huge hunks of freshly baked bread. To finish: the banoffee trifle, which was nice but perhaps a little too rich for my taste.

Despite this, a great meal and an excellent price. Highly recommended!

Now it's your turn!

Can you find six typical features of recounts and reports in extracts A and B? The first one has been done for you.

1. *Both texts show navigational aids; A has a main heading and sub-headings, B has a main heading.*
2. _____
3. _____
4. _____
5. _____
6. _____

f) Instructions

Instructional texts, such as timetables, recipes, manuals and rules, tell a reader how to do something. In order to give this information clearly, instructions usually consist of short sentences that are arranged in a numbered or stepped sequence. They use direct, functional language and can include diagrams to illustrate each step.

Certain forms of instructional text have their own recognisable features. Instructions for a sewing pattern or DIY project, for example, will mainly consist of pictures and diagrams accompanied by small sections of text. In comparison, a timetable will present a lot of numerical information in a grid.

Key Facts

Instructions:
- tell you how to do something
- use formal, direct, impersonal language; each sentence starts with an imperative verb
- are written in short sentences
- often include technical or subject-specific terms
- can include time connectives (such as 'first' and 'finally')
- often show diagrams or charts to illustrate each step
- are often arranged using bullet points or numbered lists
- can use headings to separate different stages of a sequence.

Let's have a look at two examples of instructional text.

A
1. Switch on the printer.
2. Turn the paper size key clockwise until the correct size of paper is selected, and push the lever forward at the same time.
3. Place a sheet of paper in the paper hold.
4. Push the start button.
5. Do not remove paper until printing is complete.

B **Stage 2 The cheesy mash**
- First, place the drained potatoes in a bowl.
- Mash well until mixture is smooth.
- Next, add the cream and pepper and stir.
- Then, sprinkle the grated cheese on top.
- Place under a hot grill until the cheese is bubbling.
- Finally, serve with the stuffed peppers.

Now it's your turn!

Can you find six typical features of instructional texts in extracts A and B? The first one has been done for you.

1. *Both texts show instructions in a sequence; A is a numbered list, B uses bullet points.*
2. _____
3. _____
4. _____
5. _____
6. _____

g) Letters

Letters can be written for a wide range of purposes and readers. They can be factual or fictional, formal or informal, and can be used to explain, enquire, complain, and so on. As a result, letters can be written in several different styles but usually the writer's address and the date are included and the main content is presented as continuous text.

Certain types of letter have recognisable features. Formal letters (a letter of complaint to the local council, for example) are written in a direct, firm tone and are clearly structured in short paragraphs. They are often typed and use formal forms of address at the start, such as 'Dear Sir/Madam' or 'To whom it may concern', and at the end, such as 'Yours sincerely' or 'Yours faithfully'. Informal letters (such as a note to a friend recounting a recent holiday) are often handwritten using a more chatty, casual style. They can place all of the main content in one paragraph and usually have more informal greetings, such as 'Hi!', 'Hello you!', and endings, such as 'Love and best wishes' or 'Bye for now'.

Key Facts

Letters:
- can cover a wide range of themes
- can be formal or informal; requiring different forms of greeting and ending
- usually show the writer's name or address details in the top right-hand corner
- include the date below the writer's address
- may include the recipient's name and address on the left-hand side
- are usually written in the present tense and in the first person
- may explain the purpose of writing in clear, well-structured paragraphs (formal) or in one long paragraph (informal)
- should always be signed by (or on behalf of) the writer
- often include abbreviations at the bottom: 'Enc' (short for enclosure) to show that other items have been sent with the letter; 'P. S.' (stands for postscript) to include an additional point that has been omitted in the main content.

Let's look at two examples of letters.

A

> 186 Halfpenny Lane
> Ashford Carbonell
> S17 4TX
> 01/08/07
>
> Hi Esther,
>
> How are you? Thanks for your last letter.
> I would love to stay over at Christmas.
> We break up on the 21st – does this suit you?
> I can't believe I'm even making plans
> for Christmas when the weather is so hot,
> but no doubt it will soon be upon us!
>
> Write back soon and tell me all of your news.
>
> Love
> Tilly xxxx
>
> P. S. Love to the family!

B

> Ms Matilda Moseley
> 186 Halfpenny Lane
> Ashford Carbonell
> S17 4TX
>
> Mr S Crockett
> The Writing School
> School Lane
> Chester
> CH4 5XX
>
> 1st August 2007
>
> Dear Mr Crockett
>
> I am writing in reference to the job vacancy you have advertised in the Shropshire Post.
>
> I enclose my CV, as requested, and look forward to hearing further from you.
>
> Yours sincerely
>
> M Moseley
>
> Matilda Moseley (Ms)
>
> Enc

Now it's your turn!

Can you find six typical features of letters in extracts A and B? The first one has been done for you.

1. *Both texts use abbreviated terms; A has a 'P. S.' and B has 'Enc' indicating that other items are enclosed.*
2. _____
3. _____
4. _____
5. _____
6. _____

Top Tip

Reading widely is the best way to become familiar with the range of writing styles, layouts, and features that can be used in different types of text. Remember, the faster you can work out where an extract may have come from, the easier it will be to answer a range of questions.

> ✓ **Parent Tip**
>
> *Try to make sure your child has as many opportunities as possible to examine different sources. Talk about the ways in which stories, poems, newspaper reports, recipes, textbooks, web site material, games' instructions and so on have been written. How are they laid out? What features do they include and why? Even listening to TV or radio news bulletins can help a child hear how formal, impersonal language is used to explain or recount information.*

Now that you are more familiar with where comprehension extracts may come from, let's have a look at the range of questions that could be asked about them.

2 Understand the question

Comprehension questions require a variety of skills depending upon the type of question. The examiner will be looking to assess specific skills through a range of questions, so reading each question carefully will allow you to work out the type of question being asked. For example, a question could be based on your ability to:

- *reorganise and select information*
- *find, deduce and infer information*
- *express a personal opinion*
- *compare two or more given sets of information.*

Questions can also test your general knowledge as well as your word knowledge and understanding of grammar.

Let's have a brief look at some examples of the most common question types by reading the following extract and then comparing the groups of questions below.

> Joe works for Chester Zoo and has been there now for just under six years. He began on a school work experience placement and has remained working there since he left school. Joe is a feeding assistant and his favourite job is working in the bat house. "Bats are my favourite creatures because they are so misunderstood," said Joe. "Fruit bats (also known as flying foxes) require many
> 5   types of fruit such as pineapples, mangoes and figs although they also eat pollen and some leaves. Most of their liquid intake is through fruit."
>
> Joe finds it strange that people are scared of these little nocturnal creatures. "People so rarely see them but their night vision is so good. They have adapted their mainly tropical habitats to live as free from predators as possible, which is good news for bats, but sad for those who want to see
> 10   them in their natural environments."
>
> If you have considered working with animals, local zoos are an excellent way of gaining experience because they often rely on voluntary workers.

Here are some examples of questions that could be set based on this extract:

Reorganise and select information
1. What does a fruit bat eat?   [1]
2. Where does Joe work?   [1]

Apply word knowledge and grammar
3. What does 'nocturnal' mean?   [2]
4. Is 'pollen' (line 5) a verb, noun, adverb or adjective?   [1]

Find, deduce and infer information

5 Why do fruit bats have such good night vision? ☐ 3

6 How old do you think Joe is? Explain your answer. ☐ 2

Prepare a knowledge-based response

7 Why do zoos need to rely on voluntary workers? ☐ 3

8 Name another two nocturnal creatures. ☐ 2

Introduce personal opinion

9 Imagine that you are going to have some work experience. Where would you like to go and why? ☐ 5

10 What do you think the aim of this text is? Is it successful? Explain your answer with reference to the text. ☐ 5

Compare texts

11 How are the first half of paragraph 1 and the closing sentence of paragraph 2 similar? ☐ 5

12 Why do you think the writer has included reference to bats in both paragraphs? ☐ 5

We can see that the questions begin with a fairly simple and straightforward format and are only worth one or two marks. For these questions, a careful reading of the text will find all of the information required to answer them. They are testing your ability to retrieve and organise the given information accurately.

As the question types progress, notice how external knowledge or personal opinion would also be required in order to answer the questions fully. These questions usually carry more marks and they will often ask you to support your point of view with quotes from the text.

So there are a range of questions that could be set, and the type of question asked will determine the sort of answer that you need to give. Let's look in more detail at each of these question types.

> **! Top Tip**
>
> Making sure you have understood what type of answer a question requires is a good start for writing a full and accurate answer and gaining maximum marks. The main reason pupils fail to get a high enough mark is because they have not answered the question fully. Reading and understanding the question underpins the whole test.

● Reorganise and select information

▶ Skills checklist

Reorganising and selecting information questions test whether you can:

☐ understand the meaning of a text

☐ understand and interpret key pieces of information

☐ select, describe or find information from the text

☐ show your knowledge of sentence structure and order

☐ summarise part of a text.

Here are some of the formats that this type of question can take:

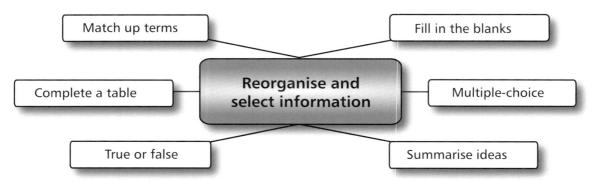

Many of these questions should be quite straightforward to answer – as long as you can find the relevant section in the text. Others may require you to assess given information and think about it logically in order to find the correct answer. Questions of this type often appear towards the beginning of a comprehension test. They are typically worth one or two marks each, usually requiring one or two words or a few lines at most, and are likely to form some of the easiest marks on the exam paper!

To find the answers to reorganising and selecting information questions it helps, though it isn't vital, if you understand the comprehension text. However, it is more important that you can:

- *recognise what information is needed to answer each question*
- *find the keywords in the text*
- *apply the right piece of text to each question.*

Finally, as all the details you will need to answer reorganising and selecting information questions are in the text, try not to leave out any questions.

Read the following report and the examples of reorganising and selecting information questions that follow. One of the answers in each example has been worked through so you can see how the answer to each type of question can be found.

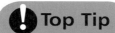 **Top Tip**

Highlighting possible keywords as you read through a comprehension text for the first time will save you time when you come to answer the questions.

Dudley and the Industrial Revolution

Dudley was a thriving area during the Industrial Revolution. This was a period of growth following the invention of many mechanical processes and industries and signalled a major change in Britain from jobs being in rural areas to jobs being in industrial, city areas. Dudley became known as the
5   'Capital of the Black Country', owing to its importance in industry, especially steel and mining. This created many jobs, and not just for the men.

Many women and children worked in the chain-making industry because the small chain links could be made at home and the workers were paid each week by the weight of chain links they had created. Women and children also worked in the mining industry; they would sort out the coal once the men had brought it from below ground. Women and children had to work in order to bring in a decent wage.

The canal system that ran throughout the Black Country was incredibly busy as boats carried freight from one area to another. Many communities grew up around the canals and the train lines because they provided not only a form of transport, but also a variety of jobs in manufacturing and processing.

My Black Country Roots

My family originate from Dudley, and I have found much information about them through my interest in genealogy. This is the research of family and ancestry, creating family trees that illustrate how people are related. Family research can be found through parish records in local churches and by ordering birth, marriage and death certificates from the General Records Office.

A lot of information is also available from the National Census that is completed every ten years. From the National Census, which can be viewed either online or in any local library, I found that my family were coal miners, steel workers, chain makers and boat makers.

Remembering the Past

The Internet is a valuable resource for genealogists. Even the National War Graves Commission has records of soldiers who were killed or wounded during wartime, and these can be found online. I did not realise that some of my ancestors died in both World Wars. During the First World War, they died at Gallipoli in Turkey, the Somme in France and in Belgium at Passchendaele. In the Second World War, members of my family fought at El Alamein in North Africa, Arnhem in Holland and in France at Dunkirk.

Family history is very rewarding and can be emotional at times, especially when yet another death certificate tells of the children who died of disease and the results of poverty. I think genealogy is important because it helps us not only to know who we are and who we belong to, but also tells us something about how people lived and what life was really like. It makes me realise how lucky I am to be living today.

a) Match up terms

Matching-up questions often ask you to pair up a series of sentences or ask you to identify which word or sentence goes with another group of sentences. Here is an example of this type of question based on the extract above:

1 Join the correct term with its definition.

a) the Black Country	an industry that many women took part in
b) the Industrial Revolution	used to transport cargo
c) chain making	the major industry during this time
d) steel industry	a period of growth following the invention of many mechanical processes
e) waterways	the area of the country surrounding Dudley

You know that all the information you need to answer this question is in the text. If you follow a clear, step-by-step process like the one given below, you will find the answers to this type of exercise quickly.

> 1 Read the first term.
>
> 2 Now go back to the text and highlight all the references to this term.
>
> 3 Then read through all of the definitions and find the one that fits with the information you have found in the text.

So a) in the above example could be worked through like this:

1 The Black Country
2 This term is written in lines 5, 12 and 15.
3 Line 5 states that Dudley became known as the 'Capital of the Black Country', so the correct definition for the first term must be:

a) the Black Country ⸺ the area of the country surrounding Dudley

> **Top Tip**
>
> Sometimes the terms given in the question might not use exactly the same words as those given in the text. You may need your knowledge of synonyms and word meaning to find the answers to some questions.

b) Fill in the blanks

A question may ask you to fill in the blanks, where sentences are given but important words or phrases have been missed out and you have to complete the statements. For this extract, an example of this type of question could be:

> **2** Complete the paragraph by filling in the answers in the spaces provided. [4]
>
> Genealogy is **a)** _____ .
> **b)** _____ show the links between different generations of the same family. Two sources of information are: **c)** _____
> _____ . The **d)** _____
> _____ is compiled every decade and shows details of people's livelihoods.

Again, following a stepped process is the best way to make sure you find the information you need as quickly as possible.

> 1 First, briefly read through the given sentences and think about the missing details. As you read, ask yourself what the sentences could be about and what type of information is likely to fill each gap.
>
> 2 Next, scan through the comprehension text until you find the relevant section or sections you need.
>
> 3 Now read through these sections, find the information you need and write in the missing words and phrases.

1. In the example above, the sentences seem to be talking about family history. The first sentence in the example question starts with a keyword, genealogy. As this is followed by the word 'is', it is logical to think that you need to find a definition for the term genealogy to complete the sentence.
2. In the given extract, paragraphs 4, 5, 6 and 7 are about family history.
3. The word 'genealogy' appears in the first sentence of paragraph 4 in the text.

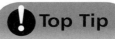

Top Tip

Looking at section headings can help you find the right part of the text quickly.

> My family originate from Dudley, and I have found much information about them through my interest in **genealogy. This is the research of family and ancestry**, creating family trees that illustrate how people are related.

The second sentence explains what this term means, so the completed first statement in the question will be:

Genealogy is **a)** *the research of family and ancestry.*

Top Tip

Pay close attention to your spelling. As all the information you need will be in the text, check that you have spelt any keywords correctly in your answers.

c) Complete a table

Some reorganising information questions may ask you to fill in gaps in a different format; you may need to complete a table, for example. Here is an example of this type of question:

3 Complete this table by adding the correct battle and country during the First and Second World Wars.

WORLD WAR I		WORLD WAR II	
BATTLE	COUNTRY	BATTLE	COUNTRY

As with the other question types in this section:

1. First read through the question and make sure you understand what you are being asked to do and what information you need to find.
2. Then find the relevant section in the text.
3. Then use the information in the text to complete the grid correctly.

B) Three steps to comprehension

1. To complete the table in this example you need to find details of the names of battles and where they took place.
2. In the given extract, the sixth paragraph includes keywords such as 'War Graves' and 'wartime', so it is likely to hold the information needed to fill in the gaps.
3. The first details to be added to the table in this example could be:

WORLD WAR I	
BATTLE	COUNTRY
Gallipoli	Turkey

d) Multiple-choice

Some select information questions will be presented in a multiple-choice format. This is where a series of options will be given and you must choose the correct one that answers the question.

Here is an example of a multiple-choice question based on the same extract.

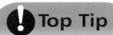

Top Tip

You may need to choose more than one option in a multiple-choice question – the number of marks available for a question can sometimes be a useful clue.

4–5 Select two responses from the options to complete the sentence correctly. [2]

Dudley was known as the 'Capital of the Black Country' because of:

a. its geographic position in the centre of the country [ ]
b. its role in mining [ ]
c. the high number of people living there [ ]
d. its role in the steel industry [ ]
e. its importance as a centre for rural jobs [ ]

The first thing to note is that this question is worth two marks because it represents questions 4–5 and it instructs you to select two correct options from the given list.

All of the information you need to answer this type of question will be in the comprehension extract. The trick is to find the relevant paragraph in the text that holds the facts you need.

In this extract, the first section heading, 'Dudley and the Industrial Revolution', shows that this is likely to be where the information needed to answer this question will be found. Reading through the first paragraph will provide you with the relevant information.

If this is then compared with the given options, the answers can be identified quickly. For example, this paragraph shows that option **b** must be one of the correct answers.

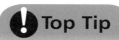

Top Tip

Check the wording of a question closely, to make sure you know what information it is asking you to find.

e) True or false

A similar question type is where questions are presented in a true-or-false format. For these questions, you may be asked to identify the correct answer by putting a tick or cross or writing the words 'true' or 'false'. Here is an example of this question type:

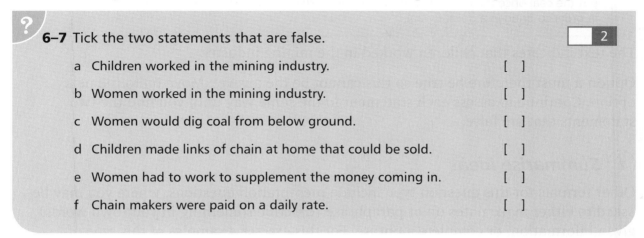

Again, all of the information needed to answer this type of question will be in the text. However, this time you will need to evaluate each statement in order to find the answer.

It can be easy to make a mistake with this type of question if you do not take the time to read each statement carefully. Follow a step-by-step system, such as the one below, to make sure you avoid making errors.

> **Top Tip**
>
> Several of the options may be either true or false, but remember, you are looking for the statements that relate to the given facts in the text.

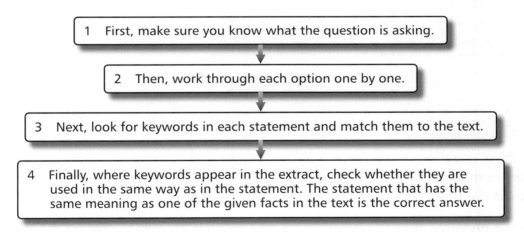

So for the above example, this process would start like this:

1. The question asks for two statements that are false.
2. Start with statement **a**: 'Children worked in the mining industry'.
3. Identify the keywords: 'children worked'. This phrase is used in lines 7 and 9.
4. Assess what option **a** states: that children worked in the mining industry. Is this what the text says?

The first sentence mentions the keywords, but not in relation to mining.

> Many women and **children worked** in the **chain-making industry** because the small chain links could be made at home and the workers paid each week by the weight of chain links they had created. Women and **children also worked in the mining industry** because they would sort out the coal once the men had brought it from below ground. Women and children had to work in order to bring in a decent wage.

The text indicates that children worked in the mining industry.

Option **a** must therefore be true so this cannot be the answer. Move on to the next option. Continue to assess each statement in the same way until you find the two statements that are false.

f) Summarise ideas

Other formats for this question type include presentation questions, where you may be asked to either make notes on or paraphrase (describe something in your own words) given information, or complete a phrase. For this extract, examples of this type of question could be:

8 Complete this phrase: The three reasons the canal system was so important are… [3]

_____

_____

_____

9 Make notes on how to find records for family history. [5]

_____

_____

_____

Both of these question variations are asking you to find the relevant facts in the text and to write them in your own words. This type of question tests whether you have understood the text and can pick out the important facts.

As with the previous question types, use a step-by-step process to answer the questions:

1. First, make sure you understand what the question is asking you to do.
2. Then, identify the sections of text that contain the facts you need to refer to in your answer.
3. Next, read the relevant details closely to find the important points.
4. Finally, use the keywords from the text to write the answer in your own words.

So for question 8:

1. The question is asking you to find three reasons for the importance of the canal system.
2. In this case, the third paragraph discusses the canal system.
3. For example: 'The canal system that ran throughout the Black Country was incredibly busy as boats carried freight from one area to another.'
4. So, the first point for this answer could be:

It allowed boats to carry freight from one area to another.

For question 9, you can follow the same process but it might be useful to structure your notes under headings, such as:

Family history record	Where it can be found

Writing notes in this format should make sure you put down all the information you need, while also helping you to avoid copying straight from the text.

Now it's your turn!

Read back through the extract and then complete questions 1–9. You may prefer to write the answers in a separate notebook.

Top Tip

Highlight keywords as you read questions and comprehension texts. This will ensure you know what you have to do and where to find the facts you need.

Apply word knowledge and grammar

Skills checklist

Word knowledge and grammar questions test whether you can:

- [ ] understand the meaning of a text
- [ ] understand and interpret key pieces of information
- [ ] select, describe or find information from the text
- [ ] show your word knowledge and spelling skills
- [ ] show your understanding of vocabulary within context
- [ ] explain a writer's use of language, grammar and literary features
- [ ] recognise the overall effects a text has on the reader
- [ ] show your knowledge of sentence structure and order.

These questions can use formats such as multiple-choice, create a table or true or false, so the information in the previous section is also useful for this type. The main difference with this form of question is that not all of the answers can be found in the text. Some will also require prior knowledge. Here are some common question types in this group:

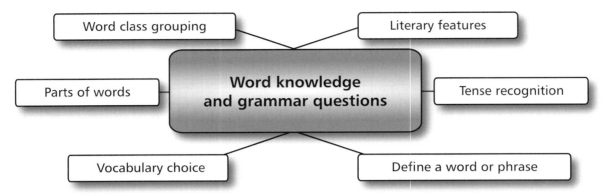

Many of these questions rely on your knowledge of grammar and spelling and on having a wide range of vocabulary. Sometimes it is possible, though, to work out an answer just by following a logical thought process.

To find the answers to word knowledge and grammar questions it helps, though it isn't vital, if you understand the comprehension text. However, as with reorganising and selecting information questions, it is more important that you are able to:

- *recognise what information is needed to answer each question*
- *find the keywords in the text*
- *apply the right piece of text to each question.*

Questions of this type often appear towards the beginning of a comprehension test and usually carry one or two marks, with definitions sometimes worth a higher score. Answers usually require only a few words, phrases or sentences so can still be grouped in the 'relatively easy' category!

Read the following letter and the examples of word knowledge and grammar questions that follow. One of the answers in each example has been worked through so you can see how the answer to each type of question can be found.

✓ Parent Tip

Reading, spelling and polishing up on grammar terms and rules will really help with these types of questions. Bond's How to do ... 11+ English *will be especially useful if your child's knowledge in these areas is not totally secure. The range of* Bond's English Assessment Papers *and the* Bond No Nonsense English *series will then help to put this knowledge into practice.*

Dear Editor,

I write in response to your recent article, 'Allotment v. Supermarket: the vegetable war'. Many people ask why we need allotments today. Allotments originated in the eighteenth century and were fundamental for the *'Dig for Victory!'* war effort, but rationing ended years ago. I think they are still
5   vitally important for a number of reasons.

Today we have a growing interest in the healthy benefits of fresh, organic food and the need to eat a balanced and varied diet. We all need to be aware of our carbon footprint and to reduce the amount of travel our food has before it reaches our door. It is also very important that wildlife has areas to flourish especially in the middle of our towns and cities. Allotments address all of these issues.

10 In my allotment this year I will be growing cabbages, cauliflowers, potatoes, leeks, parsnips and onions in the winter and sweetcorn, lettuces, beans, peas, tomatoes, carrots and marrows in the summer. In my allotment now I have a range of fruit including many berries, currants, rhubarb and apples.

As the allotment is at the bottom of my road I can walk there in a couple of minutes and bring my produce home in a wheelbarrow. No packaging, processing, advertising, shipping, canning,
15 bleaching or any other manufacturing process is necessary. Mind you, I do have to deal with a family of four fascinating and fearless foxes, who enjoy playing with my plant pots, and a hedgehog employed as my head gardener to get rid of slugs and snails. You would think that I lived in the middle of the countryside!

My allotment is a wonderful place – both relaxing and fruitful! Everyone should try it. I will
20 certainly never go back to shopping at the supermarket for fruit and veg again.

Yours

Ollie of Oxfordshire

a) Word class grouping

Word class grouping questions often ask you to identify nouns, verbs, adverbs, adjectives or pronouns within the text. Here is an example of this type of question based on the extract:

> **1–3** Look at the second sentence again: 'Many people ask why we need allotments today'. Find a:
>
> verb _____   noun _____   pronoun _____
>
> [3]

To find the answers you may find it helpful to remind yourself what a verb, noun and pronoun are:

- A **verb** is a doing or action word.
- A **noun** is a person, object, group or date.
- A **pronoun** can be used to replace a noun.

With these definitions in mind, you can then read the sentence and choose which word is the best fit for each category. So, to answer the first part of the question you need to identify a word that implies an action. Is anything happening or is someone doing something?

Yes, people are asking; **ask** is a verb.

Many **people ask** why we need allotments today.

⚠ Top Tip

You may find it useful to place the words of a sentence into columns of nouns, adjectives, verbs, adverbs, pronouns and so on depending upon what the question asks for.

B) Three steps to comprehension

b) Literary features

Questions relating to literary features often ask you to identify an example of alliteration, metaphor, simile or other literary technique. Here are two examples:

> Underline the literary feature that each phrase is an example of.
>
> **4** 'a family of four fascinating and fearless foxes':
>
> alliteration   metaphor   simile   personification   [1]
>
> **5** 'a hedgehog employed as my head gardener to get rid of slugs and snails':
>
> alliteration   metaphor   simile   personification   [1]

Ideally you will be familiar with each of the literary techniques mentioned but, even if you know what the terms mean, it can still be quite difficult to match a literary feature with an example. Below is a strategy that may help you.

Try to think of your own example for each literary feature given. You can then use these to create a template. For example:

Alliteration	Simile
She **s**ells **s**ea **sh**ells from the **s**ea **sh**ore.	It was **as** cold **as** ice.
Miss **M**ary **m**ade **m**armalade on **M**onday.	She moved **like** lightning.
Metaphor	**Personification**
The **molten gold** burned in the sky.	The **angry sky screamed** down at me.
The **man was a dog**.	The **flower winked** at me in the breeze.

Next, place the given phrase from the text underneath each example to find the best fit. Using this method, it is easier to see that the phrase stated in question 4 does not resemble a simile or metaphor and is not a form of personification. It must therefore be an example of alliteration:
'a **f**amily of **f**our **f**ascinating and **f**earless **f**oxes'.

> ✓ **Parent Tip**
>
> Look at *How to do … 11+ English* if your child needs a reminder of any of these literary techniques.

c) Tense recognition

Tense recognition is a common question type because many texts use a combination of tenses. Here is an example of this type of question in relation to the extract:

> **6** Find one sentence in the text that illustrates each of the following tenses.   [3]
>
> a) The past tense _____
>
> b) The present tense _____
>
> c) The future tense _____

A useful technique for answering this type of question is to take each sentence of the text in turn and ask yourself whether it:

- *has already happened*
- *is happening now*
- *is going to happen.*

Assessing a sentence in this way will quickly help you to determine what tense it has been written in.

Let's look at the second sentence of the given extract.

> Many people ask why we need allotments today.

Have many people already asked?	Many people **have asked** why we need allotments today.
Are many people asking now?	Many people **ask** why we need allotments today.
Are many people going to ask?	Many people **will be asking** why we need allotments today.

Which version is closest in meaning to the text? Thinking about the sentence in this way shows clearly that it is written in the present tense.

d) Define a word or phrase

Questions which ask you to define a word or phrase require more vocabulary knowledge than other question types in this group. However, if you are faced with a word or phrase you are unsure of, you can still try a range of strategies to help you work out what it means.

We briefly looked at these techniques when thinking about reading actively (pages 8–26) but we can now look at these strategies in more detail. First, let's think about how to work out the definition of an unfamiliar word.

Here are two example questions:

> **7–8** What do these words mean as used in the extract? [2]
>
> originated (line 3) _____
>
> _____
>
> fruitful (line 19) _____
>
> _____

One of the most effective techniques for working out the meaning of an unknown word is to look for a **common root**. Identifying the root should then help you to think of similar words that share the same root. If you can use this to list some familiar words then you can use their meanings to try and form a definition of the given word.

Let's have a look at how this strategy could work in relation to the first word, 'originated'.

First, try to break the word down as far as possible to see whether it contains a root word.

So 'origin' is the root of 'originated'.

At this stage, you may know what 'origin' means and be able to write down the meaning of 'originated'. If not, use this root to brainstorm other similar words. For example:

```
        original                    originally
                    origin
        originator                  originality
```

This process has led us to 'original'. This is a fairly common term that you are likely to be more familiar with. Think about its meaning. If nothing comes to mind straight away, think of occasions when you have heard or read the word. Put the term in as many different contexts as you can, as this will help you determine its meaning.

So for 'original' you might think of some of these contexts:

- I have the **original** Nintendo DS™, but my brother has the Nintendo DS™ lite.
  This means:
  I have the first version of the DS, not the latest version.
- He has an **original** way of teaching maths.
  This means:
  He has developed his own new, creative, imaginative style of teaching.
- His trainers are fake – mine are the **original** and you can tell because of this label.
  This means:
  My trainers are genuine, true and not a copy.
- She's my favourite pop star because her music is different from everyone else's – she's really **original**.
  This means:
  The pop star is different, individual, unique and unusual.

What keywords can be picked out from the meanings of these four sentences to define the word 'original'?

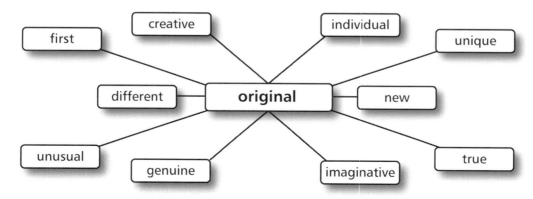

52 The secrets of Comprehension

Now, look back at the section of the extract that the question is referring to and check whether any of the keywords generated above could replace 'originated' in the given context.

> Many people ask why we need allotments today. **Allotments originated in the eighteenth century** and were fundamental for the *'Dig for Victory!'* war effort, but rationing ended years ago.

- Allotments were **first** in…
- Allotments were **creative** in…
- Allotments were **individual** in…
- Allotments were **unique** in…
- Allotments were **different** in…
- Allotments were **new** in…
- Allotments were **unusual** in…
- Allotments were **imaginative** in…
- Allotments were **genuine** in…
- Allotments were **true** in…

Many of these options could make sense in this sentence, though some of them such as 'different' would actually change the meaning of the text. The two options which seem closest in meaning to each other are 'first' and 'new'.

If allotments were first and new in the eighteenth century, they must have been **created** at this time. This logical thought process has brought us to a definition; the verb 'to originate' must mean 'to be created'.

Now let's look at how to define the meaning of a whole **phrase** which is unfamiliar to you.

9 What do you think is meant by the following phrases as used in the extract? **4**

a 'that wildlife has areas to flourish' (lines 8–9)

_____
_____
_____

b 'or any other manufacturing process' (line 15)

_____
_____
_____

When the meaning of a difficult or unfamiliar phrase is not directly given in the text, try breaking it down and looking at it in smaller chunks. First, look at the individual words you are unsure of and then place them back in the context of the sentence.

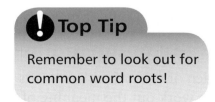

Top Tip

Remember to look out for common word roots!

In question **a** above for example, words such as 'wildlife' and 'flourish' may be unfamiliar. To work out what the whole phrase means, start by thinking about each of these words in turn.

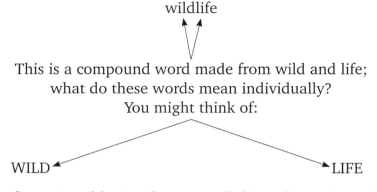

So 'wildlife' is likely to mean animals or plants that are uncontrolled or untamed and that live in a natural environment.

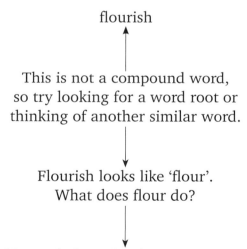

Could 'flourish' have a similar meaning? Could it mean to increase or make bigger, to grow and give more substance?

Now that you have looked at each of the unfamiliar words separately, try putting them into the context of the extract to work out the meaning of the given phrase. You might find it helpful at this stage to follow this four-step process:

PRACTICE TEST 3
Comprehension

Read the instructions carefully.

- Do not begin the test or open the booklet until told to do so.
- Work as quickly and as carefully as you can.
- You may write your answers in pen or pencil.
- You may make notes next to the extracts or on a separate sheet of paper.
- If you make a mistake, cross it out and write the new answer clearly.
- You will have 40 minutes to complete the test. It is advisable to spend the first few minutes reading through the extracts before answering any questions.

Text © Michellejoy Hughes 2007

The right of Michellejoy Hughes to be identified as author of this work has been asserted by her in accordance with the Copyright, Designs and Patents Act 1988.

All rights reserved. No part of this publication may be reproduced or transmitted in any form or by any means, electronic or mechanical, including photocopy, recording or any information storage and retrieval system, without permission in writing from the publisher or under licence from the Copyright Licensing Agency Ltd, of Saffron House, 6–10 Kirby Street, London, EC1N 8TS.

Any person who commits any unauthorised act in relation to this publication may be liable to criminal prosecution and civil claims for damages.

Published in 2007 by:
Nelson Thornes Ltd, Delta Place, 27 Bath Road
CHELTENHAM GL53 7TH, United Kingdom

07 08 09 10 11 / 10 9 8 7 6 5 4 3 2 1

A catalogue record for this publication is available from the British Library

ISBN 978 0 7487 8480 6

Page make-up by GreenGate Publishing Services, Tonbridge, Kent

Printed and bound in Croatia by Zrinski

Published by Nelson Thornes. Nelson Thornes is an Infinitas Learning company, and is not associated in any way with NFER-Nelson.

Name: _____

DATE		
SCORE OUT OF 50		
PERCENTAGE (%)		

For guidance on how best to use this test paper and for answers, please see **Bond's The secrets of Comprehension.**

Read the extract, then answer the questions that follow.

Hawk Roosting

I sit in the top of the wood, my eyes closed.
Inaction, no falsifying dream
Between my hooked head and hooked feet:
5   Or in sleep rehearse perfect kills and eat.

The convenience of the high trees!
The air's buoyancy and the sun's ray
Are of advantage to me;
And the earth's face upward for my inspection.

10 My feet are locked upon the rough bark.
It took the whole of Creation
To produce my foot, my each feather:
Now I hold Creation in my foot

Or fly up, and revolve it slowly –
15 I kill where I please because it is all mine.
There is no sophistry in my body:
My manners are tearing off heads –

The allotment of death.
For the one path of my flight is direct
20 Through the bones of the living.
No arguments assert my right:

The sun is behind me.
Nothing has changed since I began.
My eye has permitted no change.
25 I am going to keep things like this.

Ted Hughes

1 Why is the text called 'Hawk Roosting'?

_____
_____

2 Give a synonym for each of these words as they are used in the text.

  a rehearse (line 5) _____   **b** bark (line 10) _____

3 What style of text is this? Explain your answer.

_____
_____
_____
_____

PRACTICE TEST 2
Comprehension

Read the instructions carefully.

- Do not begin the test or open the booklet until told to do so.
- Work as quickly and as carefully as you can.
- Each question will tell you what type of answer is required (for example, underlined, ticked or written).
- You may write your answers in pen or pencil.
- You may make notes next to the extracts or on a separate sheet of paper.
- If you make a mistake, cross it out and write the new answer clearly.
- You will have 50 minutes to complete the test. It is advisable to spend the first few minutes reading through the extracts before answering any questions.

Text © Michellejoy Hughes 2007

The right of Michellejoy Hughes to be identified as author of this work has been asserted by her in accordance with the Copyright, Designs and Patents Act 1988.

All rights reserved. No part of this publication may be reproduced or transmitted in any form or by any means, electronic or mechanical, including photocopy, recording or any information storage and retrieval system, without permission in writing from the publisher or under licence from the Copyright Licensing Agency Ltd, of Saffron House, 6–10 Kirby Street, London, EC1N 8TS.

Any person who commits any unauthorised act in relation to this publication may be liable to criminal prosecution and civil claims for damages.

Published in 2007 by:
Nelson Thornes Ltd, Delta Place, 27 Bath Road
CHELTENHAM GL53 7TH, United Kingdom

07 08 09 10 11 / 10 9 8 7 6 5 4 3 2 1

A catalogue record for this publication is available from the British Library
ISBN 978 0 7487 8480 6

Page make-up by GreenGate Publishing Services, Tonbridge, Kent

Printed and bound in Croatia by Zrinski

Published by Nelson Thornes. Nelson Thornes is an Infinitas Learning company, and is not associated in any way with NFER-Nelson.

Name: _____

DATE		
SCORE OUT OF 50		
PERCENTAGE (%)		

*For guidance on how best to use this test paper and for answers, please see **Bond's The secrets of Comprehension**.*

Read the extract, then answer the questions that follow.

Miss Haversham had settled down, I hardly knew how, upon the floor, among the faded bridal relics with which it was strewn. I took advantage of the moment – I had sought one from the first – to leave the room, after beseeching Estella's attention to her, with a movement of my hand. When I left, Estella was yet standing by the great chimney-piece, just as she had stood
5 throughout. Miss Haversham's grey hair was all adrift upon the ground, among the other bridal wrecks, and was a miserable sight to see.

It was with a depressed heart that I walked in the starlight for an hour and more, about the court-yard, and about the brewery, and about the ruined garden. When I at last took courage to return to the room, I found Estella sitting at Miss Haversham's knee, taking up some stitches in one of
10 those old articles of dress that were dropping to pieces, and of which I have often been reminded since by the faded tatters of old banners that I have seen hanging up in cathedrals. Afterwards, Estella and I played cards, as of yore – only we were skilful now, and played French games – and so the evening wore away, and I went to bed.

I lay in that separate building across the court-yard. It was the first time I had ever lain down to
15 rest in Satis House, and sleep refused to come near me. A thousand Miss Havershams haunted me. She was on this side of my pillow, on that, at the head of the bed, at the foot, behind the half-opened door of the dressing-room, in the dressing-room, in the room overhead, in the room beneath – everywhere. At last, when the night was slow to creep on towards two o'clock, I felt that I absolutely could no longer bear the place as a place to lie down in, and that I must get
20 up. I therefore got up and put on my clothes, and went out across the yard into the long stone passage, designing to gain the outer court-yard and walk there for the relief of my mind. But, I was no sooner in the passage than I extinguished my candle; for, I saw Miss Haversham going along it in a ghostly manner, making a low cry. I followed her at a distance, and saw her go up the staircase. She carried a bare candle in her hand, which she had probably taken from one
25 of the sconces in her own room, and was a most unearthly object by its light. Standing at the bottom of the staircase, I felt the mildewed air of the feast-chamber, without seeing her open the door, and I heard her walking there, and so across into her own room, and so across again into that, never ceasing the low cry. After a time, I tried in the dark both to get out, and to go back, but I could do neither until some streaks of day strayed in and showed me where to lay my hands.
30 During the whole interval, whenever I went to the bottom of the staircase, I heard her footstep, saw her light pass above, and heard her ceaseless low cry.

Charles Dickens, **'Great Expectations'**

1 Tick the two statements that are true:
- **a** The writer had never been to Satis House before. ☐
- **b** Estella is not the narrator. ☐
- **c** The writer is good at playing cards. ☐
- **d** Miss Haversham is a ghost. ☐
- **e** The writer returned to the room after an hour. ☐

2 Find an example of each of the following parts of speech in this sentence:

'When I left, Estella was yet standing by the great chimney-piece, just as she had stood throughout.'

- **a** a conjunction _____
- **b** a preposition _____
- **c** an adjective _____
- **d** a pronoun _____

3 Explain what is on the floor in Miss Haversham's room.
_____
_____

4 Explain the meaning of each phrase as it is used in the extract.

   a 'a most unearthly object' (line 25)
_____
_____

   b 'the mildewed air' (line 26)
_____
_____

   c 'streaks of day strayed in' (line 29)
_____
_____

5 What do you think a sconce is? (line 25)
_____
_____

6 Find a phrase in each of the sections indicated below, which shows that this extract is not taken from a modern text.

   a lines 3–4 _____
   b lines 12–13 _____
   c lines 14–16 _____
   d lines 20–22 _____

7 Is the writer enjoying his stay at Satis House? Refer to the text in your answer.
_____
_____
_____
_____
_____
_____
_____
_____
_____

PLEASE TURN OVER

8 Find four homophones in this sentence. Write them, with their homophone partners, below.

'During the whole interval, whenever I went to the bottom of the staircase, I heard her footstep, saw her light pass above, and heard her ceaseless low cry.'

a _____ / _____ b _____ / _____

c _____ / _____ d _____ / _____

9 Look again at lines 14–31. How does the author make this passage seem frightening and full of suspense? Quote from the passage and explain your answer.

10 Use a maximum of 150 words to continue the story. Try to be creative but stay close to the writing style.

END OF TEST

4 Who is the narrator? Support your answer with evidence from the text.

___

5 Why do you think the writer has written the text from this viewpoint?

___

6 Explain the following phrases as used in the text:

   a 'The convenience of the high trees!' (line 6)

___

   b 'The air's buoyancy' (line 7)

___

   c 'Now I hold Creation in my foot' (line 13)

___

   d 'There is no sophistry in my body:' (line 16)

___

7 '… the earth's face upward…'. What literary technique is this phrase an example of?

8 According to the text, what makes hawks successful hunters?

9 What is the hawk's attitude? Explain your answer with reference to the text.

10 'Hawks are nothing more than vicious killers and should be eradicated.'
Do you agree with this statement? Explain your answer.

END OF TEST

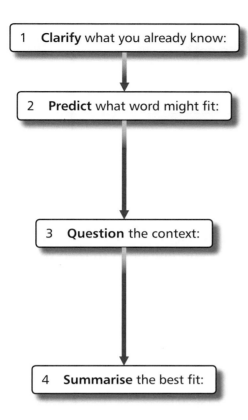

So far, it seems that the first part of the phrase means: 'Animals and plants can be untamed and uncontrolled'.

This is where your knowledge of words and word meaning is useful. Which words might make sense at the end of this phrase? Animals and plants can be untamed and uncontrolled and have areas to 'increase? Make bigger? Grow? Give more substance?'

Use your logic skills to work out which word fits best in the context. What does the paragraph tell you or imply? 'It is also very important that wildlife has areas to flourish especially in the middle of our towns and cities.' Is this saying that in cities and towns, animals and plants need an area of their own in order to survive?

Apply your chosen words and meanings to see whether your explanation of the phrase makes sense. If it doesn't, repeat the process until you have a phrase that you think makes sense. In this example, it seems logical to conclude that the phrase '… that wildlife has areas to flourish…' means 'that wild animals and plants have areas where they can grow in size and strength'.

✓ Parent Tip

Encourage your child to follow this process of Clarify, Predict, Question and Summarise by playing an 'Exchange a word' game. Try giving your child a sentence that uses a word they are unfamiliar with. Be sure to include a reasonable amount of context to help them work out the meaning. For example, "I've wasted hours in that queue and feel cantankerous*," or "It is so hot outside I'm surprised you are not* dehydrated.*"*

e) *Vocabulary choice*

Vocabulary choice questions form an important part of many comprehension tests. Here are two examples of this type of question, based on the extract:

10 Which two phrases are used to show the need to be aware of our changing climate? [2]

_____

_____

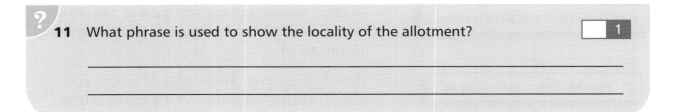

In comparison to some more complex questions, vocabulary choice questions may appear quite simple when you first read them. You might assume that all you need to do is find the matching phrase in the text and write it in. Unfortunately, these questions may not be as straightforward to answer as they first seem. Very often the phrasing used in the question paraphrases the content in the extract, rather than taking direct quotes from the text. This means sentences will have been rephrased and you will need to read the questions and the original text carefully to find the answer.

Let's look at how you might approach question 10.

The extract does not include the term 'changing climate' so we need to think about what this phrase means and what it might be referring to. Have you heard the phrase before? What other keywords have you heard used or read about in the context of climate change?

It can be helpful to note down your ideas in a flow chart or spider diagram as shown below.

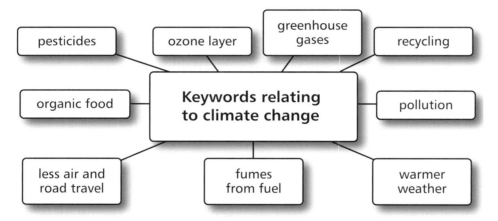

You may already have highlighted the keywords in the text when you first read through the extract. If so, you can now look through the words and phrases you have highlighted and check whether anything relates to climate change. If you haven't indicated where the keywords are in the text, reread the extract, keeping your ideas about climate change in your mind, and look for any similar words or phrases.

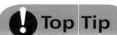

Remember, the terms used in a question might not be exactly the same words as those given in the text. You may need your knowledge of synonyms and word meaning to find the answers to some questions.

A close reading of the text should have shown that there is one sentence that relates to our need to be aware of the changing climate. Look closely at the second paragraph in the text to find the two phrases that answer question 10.

(f) Parts of words

Questions that focus on parts of words require you to understand how word roots, prefixes and suffixes work. However, they are also a test of your spelling skills. Here are some examples:

12 a The word 'ship' appears in the extract with the suffix '-ing' added. [ ] 2
A particular grammar rule must have been applied before this suffix could be added. Find two other words in the passage that follow this pattern for the '-ing' suffix.

_____   _____

  b What is the grammar rule? [ ] 2

_____

_____

_____

13 Write the common root of each word. [ ] 4

  a rationing _____   c manufacturing _____

  b varied   _____   d vitally   _____

These questions rely on your knowledge of how words are formed and how the spelling of a root word can change when a prefix or suffix is added. Let's have a look at question 12 and a strategy for solving it.

First, find the word that the question refers to. In the case of this example, the word you are looking for starts with 'ship' and ends in '-ing'. The word must be 'shipping' on line 14.

Now look closely at how this word has been formed. What happened to the root word when the suffix was added?

ship + ing   becomes   shi**p**ping

A second **p** has been added between the root word and the suffix.

The question tells you that two more words in the passage have been formed with the same suffix and that they follow the same rule as shipping. To find them you need to read back through the text and note down all the words that end in '-ing'.

You may find it useful to note down all the possible words in a grid, like the one that has been started below. This will make it easier to see where each word fits. When two more words appear in both columns, like shipping, these should be the terms you are looking for.

Double letter words	'-ing' endings
(ship) shipping	shipping
	rationing

(B) Three steps to comprehension

Once you have found both words, you need to think about the grammar rule that they all follow. The clue will be in how the root words and the suffix are connected. Be careful though – at first glance some words may look as if they follow the rule. Think hard about your spelling of root words.

Now it's your turn!

Read back through the extract and complete questions 1–13. You may prefer to write the answers in a separate notebook.

Parent Tip

If your child is unsure about any of the core spelling, grammar or punctuation rules (or common exceptions), help them to revise these by working through the relevant sections in How to do ... 11⁺ English. *See the Additional resources section of Appendix C for details.*

Find, deduce and infer information

Skills checklist

Questions that require you to find, deduce or infer information test whether you can:

- ☐ understand the meaning of a text
- ☐ understand and interpret key pieces of information
- ☐ select, describe or find information from the text
- ☐ show your word knowledge
- ☐ show your understanding of vocabulary within context
- ☐ give your opinion of a text
- ☐ explain a writer's use of language, grammar and literary features
- ☐ use clues from the text to predict what will happen next.

These are the main elements that questions in this group can be focused on:

| Deduction and reasoning: using logic and reason to reach a conclusion. | ← **Find, deduce and infer information** → | Semantics: the meaning of words, phrases, sentences or text. |

You will find some of the facts needed to answer these questions within comprehension texts. However, some questions will require you to draw on your knowledge of context and word meaning. Others will also rely on your ability to 'read between the lines' and to develop your own conclusions.

As these questions require a more detailed thought process, they generally require longer answers, of one or more paragraphs. Typically, they carry more marks and are often found towards the middle or end of a comprehension exercise.

The secrets of Comprehension

Read this extract from a school road safety project and the questions that follow. As before, questions have been worked through to show useful techniques for tackling these question types.

> 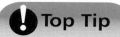 **Top Tip**
>
> As these questions require more thoughts and ideas, it is vital that you keep the question in mind as you write. It is easy to begin well and then veer off at a tangent, so make sure your answer stays on track and does what the question asks for.

How safe are our roads?

Road safety is incredibly important today when the roads are busier than ever. Some school clothing manufacturers now have 'Be Safe, Be Seen' fluorescent patches on shoes, bags and clothes. Many schools run a bicycle proficiency course where pupils can take in their bicycles and have lessons in how to ride them better and learn how to become responsible cyclists. Some schools have a crocodile walking system, where pupils are collected from their homes and create a walking chain, all holding hands for safety.

Even those pupils who are taken to school by car are encouraged to arrive and leave safely. Yellow lines are usually painted on the road outside a school entrance to stop parents parking there, and many schools have a crossing patrol person who will lead them safely across the road or to a car park where parents can wait in a safe place.

Television adverts reinforce the message that car drivers are less likely to cause a death if they hit a child at 30 miles per hour than if they drive at 40 miles per hour. Speed cameras and speed signs are also used to prompt drivers to slow down and to take care when driving. Ultimately we need to teach our children to always be aware and to take great care near roads. Drivers must be reminded that they have a responsibility to look after children by watching their speed, especially in residential areas where accidents are prevalent.

a) Deduction and reasoning

Some questions in this group will require you to use your powers of deduction in order to come to a conclusion about what you have read. This means that you need to read the text carefully, think about it in relation to the question and then use your understanding to make a decision.

Here are two examples of this type of question based on the extract above:

1 Give three road safety benefits of a crocodile walking system. [3]

2 Give three road safety benefits of television advertising. [3]

_____

_____

_____

As with all comprehension questions, you must first make sure you understand what the question is asking and that you have highlighted any keywords it uses. Then find the section in the extract that mentions these keywords and think about how this part of the text relates to the question.

To be awarded full marks in questions like this, it is likely that you will need to think beyond the information that the comprehension text gives you. In a way, you can think of the text as a springboard that should lead you to other ideas.

Let's look at how you could work out the answer to question 1 above.

Give three **road safety benefits** of a **crocodile walking system**.

keywords

The question is asking you to think about how a crocodile walking system can provide road safety benefits. Before you can list any benefits, you must understand what a crocodile walking system is. Go back to the text and read lines 7–8, which talk about the crocodile walking system. Use this information to answer questions such as:

Who uses this system?

- Children (pupils)

What does it involve?

- Collecting children from their home
- Walking to school in a line (chain)
- Holding hands

Asking questions like these, helps to highlight the features of the system. So, what benefits would a system like this provide?

Brainstorm as many ideas as you can think of. You may find it useful to note your thoughts down in a spider diagram, like the one below.

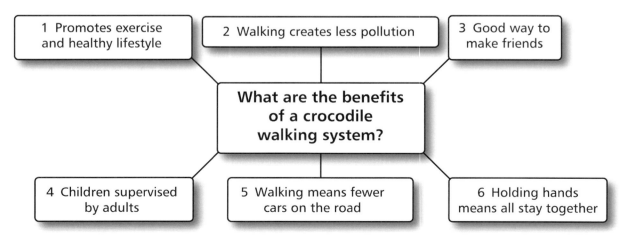

The secrets of Comprehension

These all seem possible benefits of a system like this, but remember: the question asks you to write specifically about **road safety** benefits. The first three benefits listed above are not really to do with road safety. So consider the other three benefits – can they be developed further?

How could supervising children on their way to school promote road safety?	What road safety benefit could fewer cars on the road lead to?	Why might holding hands be helpful in terms of road safety?
If someone is walking with them, children will be warned to pay more attention to what is around them, such as vehicles, road signs and pedestrian crossings.	If there are fewer cars on the road, this may help to reduce the number of road accidents.	If children are holding hands it will make them less likely to run off, possibly into the road.

These ideas answer the question, as they show some of the road safety benefits of a crocodile walking system. Following this example through, you can see that you need to use a more in-depth process of deduction and think 'outside' the information given in the text, in order to find the answer to this type of question.

✓ Parent Tip

When questions become more abstract, it is easy to lose focus and can be difficult to get back into a flow of thought. Try this game to help improve your child's ability to focus, to think quickly and effectively and to work without distraction.
- *Write out the alphabet, one letter per line, vertically down a sheet of paper.*
- *Think of as many first names as possible in five minutes; award 2 points for the initial name on each line and then 1 point for each additional one.*
- *The aim is to score as highly as possible within the time frame.*
This game can be varied; try it with food, drinks, animals, places, brand names, shops and so on.

Questions where you need to deduce or infer an answer can also be presented in a multiple-choice format. As for all questions in this format, you must choose the correct answer from a set of given options. However, for this version of multiple-choice you will need to assess how the options relate to the information that is given in the text. The answer is likely to be inferred or implied, rather than being stated in the extract directly.

Look at these example questions in relation to the given extract.

3 According to the article, what is the single most important way in which we can ensure children are safe on the roads?

    a Encourage more bicycle proficiency courses to run in schools. [ ]

    b Children must learn the need for awareness and caution. [ ]

    c Paint more yellow lines outside school entrances. [ ]

    d Ensure we have more crocodile walking systems. [ ]

    e Have more speed cameras and speed signs for drivers. [ ]

4 According to the article, how can drivers improve road safety? [1]

   a Use public transport more regularly. [ ]

   b Avoid driving in residential areas. [ ]

   c Avoid parking on the yellow lines outside a school entrance. [ ]

   d Check their speed when driving. [ ]

   e Watch more television adverts about road safety. [ ]

Let's look at how you could work out the answer to question 3.

Any of the options may seem possible when you first read through them, as they all show ways in which children's safety near roads can be improved.

The clue is in the use of three keywords in the question. You need to find the one option that gives the 'single most important' method. What does this mean in relation to the comprehension text?

First, think of as many synonyms or similar phrases as you can for the keywords.

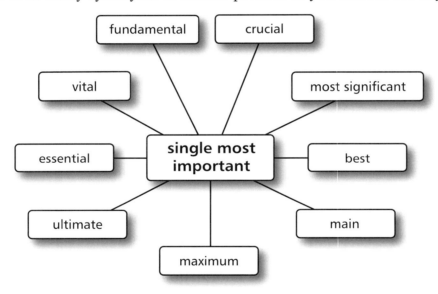

Now scan back through the extract, looking for keywords that are similar to any of the synonyms you have thought of.

In this example, the penultimate (last but one) sentence states:

> Ultimately we need to teach our children to always be aware and to take great care...

'Ultimately' is a similar term to the synonyms found for the phrase 'single most important'.

Compare this statement with each of the multiple-choice options. Is it similar in meaning to one option? Yes, option **b** states that children must learn awareness and caution. From this, it is clear that the answer must be option **b**.

b) Semantics questions

To work out the answers to semantics questions you need to deduce information about words using your existing knowledge of word meanings. However, unlike questions that test your basic vocabulary skills, semantics questions require you to understand the wider context of the relevant phrase, sentence or paragraph, in order to determine word meaning accurately.

Look at these examples of semantics questions.

> **5** Explain why it is called 'a crocodile walking system'. ☐ 3
>
> _____
> _____
> _____
>
> **6** Explain how a 'crossing patrol person' is useful for road safety. ☐ 3
>
> _____
> _____
> _____

Let's look at the thought process needed for this type of question by working through question 5.

The meaning of this phrase is not directly given in the text, so how can you find the answer? A literal interpretation of this phrase would lead us to believe that 'a crocodile walking system' was a system that crocodiles use to help them walk. This is obviously not the correct answer!

Instead of looking at the meaning of the individual words, the crucial strategy here is to examine the phrase within the context in which it appears. Here is the relevant section of text again:

> Some schools have a crocodile walking system, where pupils are collected from their homes and create a walking chain, all holding hands for safety.

From reading this part in full, we can see that 'a crocodile walking system' relates to 'create a walking chain, all holding hands for safety'. It is clear then that the term 'a crocodile walking system' refers to the way in which some children walk to school. But this does not answer the question, as it does not explain what it has to do with crocodiles.

This is where you need to draw on your own knowledge. What do you know about crocodiles? What do you associate with them? How would you describe them? Here are some ideas you might think of:

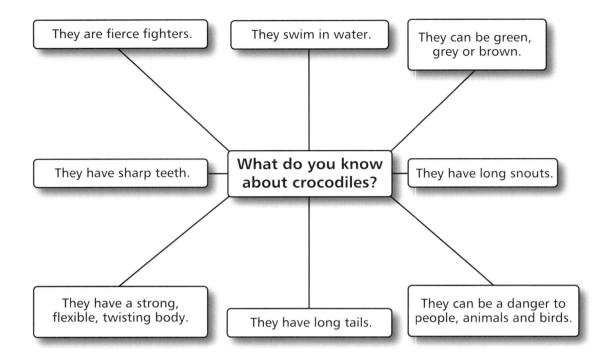

Once you have written down as many descriptors as you can think of, you need to check whether any of these details make sense when compared with the phrase in the text that explains the system: 'create a walking chain, all holding hands for safety'.

There are two descriptors that seem to fit well with the idea of a walking chain:

- *They have long tails.*
- *They have a strong, flexible, twisting body.*

A walking chain is likely to be made up of several children, so what do you think it would look like?

- *It might be quite long, like a crocodile's tail.*
- *It would be quite strong, because all of the children would be holding hands, making one chain (or body).*
- *It would be flexible and appear to twist, as each child in the chain would be able to move around obstacles or change direction when necessary.*

These points explain why this type of walking chain is called a 'crocodile walking system'. Here is a sample answer based on these points:

It is called a crocodile walking system because the chain of children could be quite long, like a crocodile's tail. The chain would also be like a crocodile's body because it would be quite strong, due to all of the children holding hands, and would be flexible, allowing children to move around obstacles or change direction easily.

Now it's your turn!

Read back through the extract and then complete questions 1–6. You may prefer to write the answers in a separate notebook.

Prepare a knowledge-based response

> ### Skills checklist
>
> *Knowledge-based response questions test whether you are able to:*
> - [ ] understand the meaning of a text
> - [ ] understand and interpret key pieces of information
> - [ ] place a text into a historical context
> - [ ] show your understanding of vocabulary within context
> - [ ] show your word knowledge and spelling skills.

In each of the question types we have examined so far, we have seen that you can either use details given in a text to answer a question completely or use an extract as a starting point to form your own ideas.

Knowledge-based questions often do not follow this format because they may not always refer directly back to the text. These are the main elements that questions in this group can focus on:

These types of question may only be loosely related to the topic, meaning you will need to draw much more on your own knowledge and logical thinking skills to find the answers required. They are often worth a higher number of marks and can therefore require you to write longer answers, ranging from a few sentences to one or two paragraphs.

Read the following extract from a radio interview transcript and the examples of knowledge-based questions that follow. As before, some examples have been worked through to highlight useful strategies for approaching this question type.

Why is music so important in my life? Well, put simply, it is one of my greatest passions. In particular, I love listening to grand musical feasts such as operas. I guess we have the Italians to thank for this wonderful form of musical drama, owing to the fact that opera originated in Italy during the late 16th century.

Naturally, it didn't take long for their neighbours to pick up on the trend. Germany, for example, opened its first public opera house in Hamburg in 1678 and at around the same time a British composer, Henry Purcell, was starting to introduce London to musical theatre. He really took up the baton for instrumental and vocal music here and his opera, Dido and Aeneas, premiered in 1689. I often wish I had been around during this period, as it must have been a tremendously exciting time for music lovers!

The magic of musical dramas, such as operas, would of course be lost without the talents of an accomplished orchestra. As I'm sure your listeners know, an orchestra is usually made up of instruments belonging to four families: the strings, the woodwind, brass and percussion. An instrument is classed as a string instrument if it makes its sound through being bowed or plucked, like a violin, cello or double bass. Woodwind instruments are usually made of wood and make

> sounds by being blown; the clarinet, flute and bassoon are popular instruments in this group. The other family that is blown is the brass – but they are all made of metal and control sound through valves, slides and buttons. The trumpet, trombone and horns are all commonly known members of this set. Lastly, there are the percussion instruments. These need to be hit to create sounds, like the tambourine, xylophone and pianoforte.
>
> I often find that the best way to explain my love of orchestral music to someone is by letting them experience it first-hand. So, I have prepared a short compilation CD that should be cued up and ready to play. I'll be interested to hear what your listeners think …

Knowledge-based questions require the ability to relate information to knowledge you already have about a topic. It may not always be easy to think of connections at first, but it can help to try and associate topics with events that have happened to you or situations you have been in.

a) Facts

Here are some examples of typical fact-based questions based on the extract above:

1 The text mentions one composer. Name three other famous composers. [3]

_____   _____   _____

2 Name one more member of each of the four musical instrument families. [4]

Strings   _____

Brass   _____

Woodwind   _____

Percussion   _____

3 Two European countries are mentioned in the text. Name three other European countries. [3]

_____   _____   _____

The answers to these questions cannot be taken directly from the text and you cannot use your reasoning skills to deduce meaning or 'read between the lines'. These questions clearly rely on the existing knowledge you are able to bring to the topic – you are therefore likely to know the answers or not.

At first glance you might think that you know nothing about composers or musical instruments and want to move straight on to the next set of questions. However, don't panic! You probably do have some knowledge about the topic; you just need to find a way to unlock it.

Let's look at how you might work towards the answer for question 1 above.

By highlighting keywords in the extract, you should have found that the only composer mentioned is Henry Purcell. As there is no more information in the text, try to brainstorm everything you know about music and composers.

Start by asking yourself a variety of questions such as:

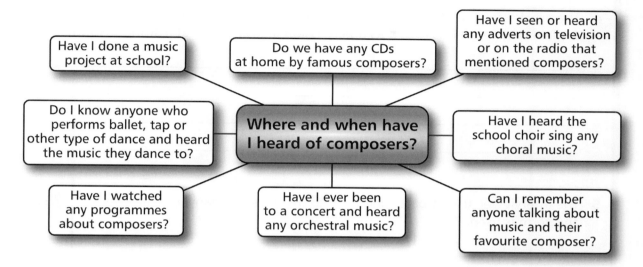

It is likely that you will have heard the names of some composers before, and asking yourself questions like these will help you to tap into your memory. With these types of questions in mind you might now recall a time when you have:

- been to the theatre and watched a musical production, such as **Andrew Lloyd Webber**'s Joseph and the Amazing Technicolor Dreamcoat or heard **Tchaikovsky**'s music in The Nutcracker or Swan Lake ballets.
- seen a cartoon that was set to music, like the animated version of **Prokofiev**'s Peter and the Wolf or **Dukas**'s The Sorcerer's Apprentice, starring Mickey Mouse, in Fantasia.
- watched Bill and Ted collect **Beethoven**, the famous composer, on their travels through time in the film, Bill and Ted's Excellent Adventure, or listened to music by **Bizet** and **Grieg** in the film Babe.
- listened to the music that accompanied a famous sporting event, such as Torvill and Dean's ice skating routine to **Ravel**'s Bolero or heard Pavarotti sing **Puccini**'s Nessun Dorma as a World Cup song.

Using this brainstorming method encourages you to think outside the information given in the text. It is one of the best strategies for generating your own knowledge and memories. In this example, the names of nine composers have come to mind – several more than is needed for the answer! Even if this technique only brings one or two things to mind, it will be better to note these down than just move straight on to the next set of questions.

 **Top Tip**

If you are not fully sure of how to spell special terms, such as the composers' names listed here, it is much better to make a best guess rather than leave a blank space.

b) Logic

Knowledge-based questions can also take the form of logic questions. Here are two examples of this version in relation to the same extract:

> **4** The article states that the pianoforte is part of the percussion family. [3]
> Explain why it can be classed as a percussion instrument, not a string instrument.
>
> _____
> _____
> _____
> _____
>
> **5** The interviewee uses a particular term to describe Germany. Explain why [2]
> this term is used.
>
> _____
> _____
> _____

Again, there is only a small amount of information in the text that will help you with these questions. To work out the answer to this type of knowledge-based question, you will need to rely on your logical thinking and reasoning skills. Try to follow a coherent and step-by-step thought process, asking yourself a series of questions as you work through each stage.

For example, you might reach the answer to question 4 by following this stepped approach:

1. First, make sure you understand what the question is asking.
2. Then, check for any unfamiliar terms. Following a strategy like the ones explained on pages 51–55 will help you to look at an unknown word separately as well as within the context of the given phrase or passage.
3. Next, ask yourself a set of related questions. This is where logical thinking comes in and you need to use your reasoning skills to find a sensible answer.
4. Finally, when you have thought logically about these questions, you can use your responses to form an answer to the question.

So for question 4:

1. The answer needs to give clear and logical reasons why the instrument fits in the percussion family, not the string family.
2. This question uses mostly familiar words and phrases, as examples of percussion and string instruments are given in the text.

3 You might ask yourself the following questions:

Q	A
What defines a string instrument?	The text states that string instruments are bowed or plucked.
What defines a percussion instrument?	The text states that percussion instruments are hit.
What is a pianoforte?	It is more commonly known as a piano.
Have I ever looked inside a piano? How does it make its sound?	A piano has strings; the strings make the sound.
What does the piano have in common with other percussion instruments?	When the piano keys are pressed, small hammers strike the strings inside; the strings are hit to produce a sound.

4 So your answer might look like this:

String instruments make their sound through being bowed or plucked. The pianoforte makes its sound by small hammers hitting the strings inside. As the strings are hit, not plucked or bowed, the pianoforte is classed as a percussion instrument.

Asking yourself questions like these may not always lead you to the answer but it is a good technique to try, because it will help you to think logically and focus on the question being asked.

Now it's your turn!

Reread the extract and then complete questions 1–5. You may prefer to write the answers in a separate notebook.

✓ Parent Tip

Wide-ranging general knowledge is the best preparation for knowledge-based questions. Whilst fiction reading is great for supporting many skills, the best method for developing general knowledge is through exploring different children's encyclopaedias, or other educational and factual children's print or electronic resources.

● Introduce personal opinion

▶ Skills checklist

Personal opinion questions test whether you can:

- ☐ understand the meaning of a text
- ☐ understand and interpret key pieces of information
- ☐ develop information from a text
- ☐ recognise a writer's aim and viewpoint
- ☐ recognise the overall effects a text has on the reader
- ☐ explain a writer's use of language, grammar and literary features
- ☐ show your understanding of vocabulary within context
- ☐ continue a piece of writing
- ☐ summarise part of a text
- ☐ use clues from the text to predict what will happen next
- ☐ give your opinion on a text
- ☐ support your comments by quoting from, or referring to, the text.

Personal response questions can take a range of different forms and each one will test your understanding of the text as well as your ability to express your own opinion. Here are three of the most common elements that a question can be based on:

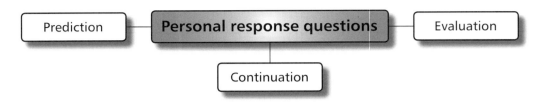

Some questions will require you to draw on your knowledge of context and word meaning whilst others will rely on your ability to 'read between the lines' and to develop your own conclusion. Several personal response questions will also ask you to support your comments with evidence from the text. You can do this by taking direct quotes from the text and stating which lines they have come from, or by paraphrasing the text.

In all cases, the text will act as a springboard for your ideas and opinions; it will not give you a direct answer. As these questions require a more detailed thought process, they generally require longer answers, of one or more paragraphs. Typically, they carry a higher level of marks and are often found towards the end of a comprehension exercise.

Read the following extract, taken from a narrative text, and the range of example questions that follow. One question of each type has been examined in detail to show you how different strategies can be used to develop an answer.

1 The Dreadful Thing

The audience began a torrent of applause and Mrs Portman peered at Solomon over the top of her gold-rimmed glasses. Solomon, however, hardly noticed. He was wondering how he could possibly need the toilet again after having been three times already. His hands were
5 clammy and sticky and his thick, black fringe was now stuck to his damp forehead. With butterflies in his stomach and feeling dizzy with fear, he knew that he had to stand up and walk over to the stage. But he couldn't. His legs refused to move and his feet were stuck fast.

The applause was dying down and Solomon could hear his own heartbeat thumping above
10 it all. "This is it," he thought. Drawing on all the strength he had, Solomon stood up and shuffled reluctantly over to the microphone. As he turned to face the audience he remembered his teacher's final words, "If you feel a bit jittery, don't look at the audience. Just look over their heads to the clock on the back wall. Then tell yourself that nobody else is in the room but you and that clock. Then begin, reading loudly and slowly so that the clock can hear you.
15 Remember to smile at the clock before you start and after you have finished."

Solomon locked onto the clock. "Don't look away from the clock," he told himself as he opened his book to the right page. Feeling very wobbly Solomon cleared his throat, smiled at the clock and then …

And then it happened. Solomon's eyes dipped and, catching sight of the sea of faces, he
20 began desperately searching for his mum and dad. But there were just too many of them. Blonde hair, red hair, brown hair, black hair, women, men, boys, girls, babies, grannies, granddads, teachers, pupils, tall people, short people, old people, young people, smiling faces, bored faces, expectant faces, excited faces … The multitude seemed never-ending, but there was still no sign of his parents.

a) Prediction

One of the most common question types in this group requires you to predict something that may happen as a result of an event, situation or explanation given in the text. These questions test whether you have fully understood the text and can analyse what the consequences of a situation or a character's actions could be. Here is a typical prediction question based on the extract above.

> **1** What do you think will happen next? [2]

In order to answer this type of question accurately, you first need to find the clues that relate to the storyline. Several of your active reading questions (see pages 8–26) should be useful here. In particular, answers to the following key questions should help you decide what might be a logical next step of the story because they focus on what is happening, when, where and why as well as on who is involved:

- Are there any characters?
- What writing style and form of text has been used?
- What is happening? When? Where? Why?
- Have you read anything like this before? What does it remind you of?
- What is the aim or purpose of the writing?

Once you have grasped these fundamental clues, look again at where the extract finishes and think about what might happen next. You may be able to think of different routes that a story could follow from this point. To map out your ideas clearly, try noting down your thoughts in a quick diagram.

The format shown below can be a successful way to follow through your ideas. For example, you might begin a diagram for this question like this:

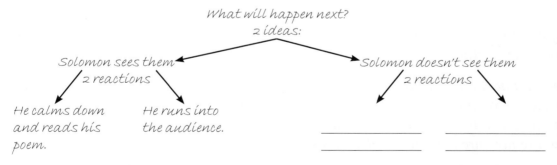

Using this technique to plot the possible progress of a story helps to make prediction much easier and it should enable you to form a logical and realistic answer. If you have worked through more than one possible outcome, you can choose which version you prefer and use it to answer the question.

One possible response to this example could therefore be:

> *I think that Solomon sees his mum and dad in the audience and this gives him the confidence that he needs. He is able to calm down and read his poem.*

Now it's your turn!

What do you think will happen next if Solomon doesn't see his parents? Write two alternative reactions in the diagram on page 71 and then use one idea to write a different version of the answer below.

_____
_____
_____

b) Continuation

A similar type of personal response question also focuses on your ability to predict what comes next, but this type requires you to draw more on your imagination and creativity. In this format you have to write a continuation of the text.

Here is an example:

 2 Write the next stage in the story. Continue the passage in the same style and write no more than 150 words.

Several points are important to remember about this type of question:

- *You must try to write in the style of the author.*
- *Your answer must continue straight on from where the extract finishes.*
- *The storyline must follow a sensible path in line with the given text.*
- *You should use a broad vocabulary and show good spelling and grammar knowledge.*
- *If a word limit or maximum extent has been given, you must keep within it.*

Many children find this type of personal response question difficult and sometimes lose marks because they:

- cannot think of what to write
- write too much and run out of space and time
- take so long thinking about what to write that they run out of time
- are not sure how to complete a piece of writing.

Again, your responses to the ten active reading questions (see pages 8–26) will give you a good head start for this type of question. Starting with these ideas, you can then follow the TEMPO strategy to structure your thoughts more clearly and develop your answer.

Let's have a look at how the TEMPO technique could work for question 2.

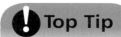 **Top Tip**

Tempo means TIME. This technique will remind you that time is important as you plan and write your answer.

Title – what is it?
- 'The Dreadful Thing'.
- It sounds as if something awful is going to happen. Could it be resolved before the end?

Environment – how does it affect the storyline and characters?
- Set in a school hall, probably during a school show.
- Quite a scary atmosphere, as there are so many people in the audience.

TEMPO

Mood – what is it and how does it change?
- Starts with a happy, expectant audience. Everyone is clapping.
- Solomon is nervous and feels worse as he gets near the microphone.
- Panic increases when he looks at the audience.

Opportunities – how could the storyline continue or change?
- The text ends with Solomon looking for his parents.
- What route could the plot take from here?
  - He finally finds his parents, calms down, reads his poem, everyone applauds, he wants to read another poem?
  - He finds his parents, still feels too nervous to read, runs to Mum and Dad, they take him home?

Plot – what is the outline and aim of the story?
- Main character: Solomon.
- Plot: He is about to perform a poem in front of a large audience. He tries to follow his teacher's advice and look at the clock. He looks down at the audience and starts scanning for his parents. Fear sets in. We are left wondering whether he will find his parents and read his poem.
- Aim: to share Solomon's struggle to get over his nerves of reading in public.

Using this technique to make notes will help you make sure that you fully understand what has happened so far and how the mood of the setting and characters is developing. You will also have clearly sketched out some ideas for how the storyline could continue and can now choose one to construct your answer.

Remember to write in the same style as the extract. This means using the same or similar vocabulary, writing in the same tense and even writing sentences to a similar length. This will help your continuation to flow on well from the given text. Also watch out for spellings, grammar, punctuation and the word limit!

Here is an example of one possible continuation:

> *They were nowhere to be found. Solomon could feel his knees shaking and as hard as he tried, he could not stop his bottom lip from trembling. His eyes swam with tears that he could no longer control. Angry sobs and wails tumbled out of his mouth and his red face dripped with tears.*

Top Tip

You could lose marks for writing too much or too little. Use the number of marks available, word limit guidance and space available to write in, to help you gauge how much to write.

Mrs Moseley stood up from the middle of the room and hurriedly moved down the central aisle as the audience looked on in sympathy. Solomon finally caught sight of his mum. The tears subsided as the little boy lifted his arms up for a comforting hug. Even with a round of applause, Solomon could not be persuaded to remain on the stage, so Mum carried him back to her seat and plonked him on Mr Moseley's lap. Solomon had learned a valuable lesson. He would never again forget to keep his eyes away from the audience!

> **Now it's your turn!**
> Try writing your own continuation of the story in your notebook. Be creative, but stay close to the writing style. Write between 130 and 150 words. Ask someone to comment on how well you have continued the story.
>
> 8

c) Evaluation

Unlike the last two question types we have looked at, evaluation questions will not ask you to continue a piece of text. Instead, typical examples of this question type will take one or more themes explored in a text and present it as a separate topic for you to discuss and offer your opinion about.

Here is an example of an evaluation question based on the same extract:

> **3** 'All children should be made to perform in public.' Do you agree with this statement? Explain your answer.
>
> 8

These questions usually introduce the subject in the form of a question or a statement (as in the example above) and will then ask for a response to the issue. They often include key terms such as 'explain' and 'discuss' and allow you to write as much as you feel you need to in order to cover all the relevant points.

Again, this is a particular question type that children often have trouble with because they:

- *are not sure what points to include*
- *find it difficult to express their own opinion*
- *do not support their points sufficiently*
- *do not draw their answer to a clear conclusion.*

As with the other question types we have looked at, if you try to approach these questions with a clear strategy and a mental checklist, it will make it easier to develop a structured argument.

The main points to remember about this type of question are that you should:

- include relevant facts and your own opinion
- refer to the text as well as your own knowledge where useful
- discuss both sides of the issue or argument clearly
- try to explain each point concisely and avoid repetition
- draw your own conclusion after presenting the facts.

Here is a good technique for answering evaluation questions:

1. First, make sure you have read the question closely and understand what it is asking you to do.

2. Next, you should make notes on points that you feel present the 'pros' and the 'cons' (the positive and negative elements) of the issue.

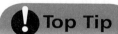

Top Tip

It can be helpful to look back at the text at this stage, as it could give you some ideas to get you started.

1 In the case of this example, it is asking you to decide whether you agree or disagree with the statement and to explain your viewpoint.

2 Writing your thoughts in a grid can help you to compare points more easily and will also make it clearer to organise them into a structured answer. For example:

Performing in public

Pros	Cons
Prepares children for similar situations, such as other school musical or drama productions, class presentations, assemblies, exams and school entry interviews.	Can put some children (like Solomon in the text) under a lot of pressure.
Shows children what it is like to be nervous.	Can be very stressful and cause problems with eating and sleeping. Could give children nightmares.
Helps children learn how to deal with nerves and develop coping skills and strategies.	Can make children suffer and this is cruel. It is not fair to force someone to do something and take away their choice.
Gives children confidence when they succeed.	Can make shy children even more shy and quiet. Could lower confidence.
Can help children discover a talent for performing.	Might put children off any kind of performing in the future.

Read through the grid when you have written down all of the points you can think of for both sides of your debate. With all of these ideas in front of you, you should find it easier to make a decision about which viewpoint you agree with the most.

Now you are ready to start writing your response. You could write an answer that states a point from one side of the argument and then follow it with a related comment from the opposite viewpoint. For example:

Positive point

If all children were made to perform in public it could help to prepare them for similar situations they might come across, for example other school productions, presenting class projects or assemblies or even interviews for secondary school. However, it could also put many children under a lot of pressure like Solomon, the main character in the text.

Negative point

However, if you wrote your whole answer in this way it could get a bit confusing for the reader and seem disjointed. Writing all about one viewpoint first, then the other and finally giving your conclusion is likely to make your argument easier to read. If you write in paragraphs, this will also help your answer to look more organised.

> **! Top Tip**
>
> To make sure you include all of the ideas you have thought of, mark off each point as you include it in your answer.

> **! Top Tip**
>
> When you swap from one side of a discussion to another, remember to link your points with connective words or phrases: 'however', 'on the one hand… but on the other hand', 'some people might think that…' , 'in comparison', 'meanwhile' and so on.

Here is an example of a possible answer based on the table of ideas above:

If all children were made to perform in public it could help to prepare them for similar situations they might come across, such as other school productions, presenting class projects or assemblies or even interviews for secondary school. It would give them the opportunity to see what it was like to be nervous and they could learn from this. They might become more used to it or develop ways of coping with the feeling. After they had performed once, it would give them confidence to do it again and they might even discover a talent for performing.

However, telling children that they have to perform in public would also put many children under a lot of pressure. It could make them feel very stressed and make them unwell. We can see this with Solomon, the main character in the text. He was so nervous that he had to keep going to the toilet, was very hot and sweaty and felt dizzy. If children are extremely worried about a performance it might even stop them from sleeping. Although the experience of performing might make some children more confident, it could make shy children even more shy and lower their confidence.

I think it would be very cruel to make children perform in public. It is not fair to force someone to do something, they should be allowed to choose whether they want to do it or not.

Now it's your turn!

Reread the report extract on pages 40–41 and then have a go at this evaluation question: 8

'What is the point of researching family history? We should look to the future not the past.'
Do you agree with this statement? Explain your answer.

Write your answer in your notebook and ask someone to comment on your response.

Compare texts

Skills checklist

Text comparison questions test whether you can:

- [ ] understand the meaning of a text
- [ ] understand and interpret key pieces of information
- [ ] select, describe or find information from the text
- [ ] recognise a writer's aim and viewpoint
- [ ] recognise the overall effects a text has on the reader
- [ ] explain a writer's use of language, grammar and literary features
- [ ] show your understanding of vocabulary within context
- [ ] give your opinion on a text
- [ ] comment on the structure, order and presentation of a text
- [ ] support your answers by quoting from, or referring to, the text.

Some comprehension test papers do not just ask questions about one extract. You may find that some of the comprehension tests you have to take will set questions around a group of two, three or even more texts. This set of materials can be chosen for any number of reasons. For example, the texts may have been written:

- about the same topic
- by the same author
- in the same era
- using the same style of writing
- using different writing styles
- in different formats (such as prose, letter, newspaper article).

Papers that are based around more than one text will incorporate many of the same question types we have explored throughout this book. You will therefore be able to use the same strategies and techniques to find the answers. The only difference is that to give full responses, you will need to focus on more than one text in your answer.

However, some comprehension question types can only be asked in relation to sets of multiple texts. These are three of the core elements that typical comparative questions can focus on:

!Top Tip

Highlighting keywords is absolutely vital when reading a set of multiple texts because you need to find the correct information quickly and efficiently. Write in the margins or at the bottom of a page to remind yourself of an important point as you read through.

Read the following extracts and the examples of comparative questions that follow. As before, questions have been worked through to show useful techniques for tackling these question types.

A   Your sweet tooth is destroying nature!

Chocolate – your seemingly harmless treat that is destroying wildlife.

The cacao bean is harvested from trees in Africa's Ivory Coast and in order to create hybrid, sun-loving trees, deforestation on a massive level has ploughed
5 *ahead unchecked.*

The cacao tree requires huge amounts of synthetic chemicals in order to resist the diseases and pests that it is prone to. These high levels of extremely toxic pesticides have contaminated the ground. Consequently, the creatures that inhabit the area are being driven out.

10 *Act now! Buy ethically produced chocolate.*

If you don't, you'll be contributing to the rapid deforestation of the rainforests and ultimately, the extinction of many species of animal and plant.

B   Chocolate – the early years

The **Aztecs** were among the first people known to have made chocolate (or cacao as it was called then, as it was made from the pods of the cacao tree). They drank a thick spicy liquid made from the cacao bean. It also contained
5 chillies and looked like blood because it was dyed dark red. Unsurprisingly, this did not suit the European palate!

In the 16th century the Spanish used cacao seeds to develop a chocolate drink that contained sugar and spices and was mixed with wine or beer. This new recipe became very popular because it was far more suited to European tastes. This drinking chocolate arrived in England in about 1655,
10 at the same time as coffee and tea.

For many years chocolate was available only as an expensive drink for the elite classes, but the arrival of the **Industrial Revolution** was to change this. New machinery made it possible to create solid bars of chocolate in large quantities. This meant that it could be sold at a much lower price to more people. The first solid chocolate bar was created in 1847 by Fry's Chocolate.

c It's official – Chocolate is good for us!

A new report published this week states that chocolate is actually good for us. The report lists the findings of a number of research studies,
5 all showing that chocolate has many beneficial effects upon our health.

According to the first section of the report, chocolate:

- does not cause acne or spots
10 - contains many ingredients that protect teeth, as opposed to causing dental cavities
- has no more sugar than many other products
- has a higher Oxygen Radical Absorption
15 Capacity value than most foods, which may help to protect the body from the effects of free radicals.

The results of a second study found that:

- a substance in cocoa helps the body
20 process nitric oxide – a compound critical for healthy blood flow and blood pressure
- dark chocolate has a high level of flavonols, which prevent fat-like substances in the bloodstream from clogging the arteries
25 and make blood platelets less likely to stick together and cause clots.

The results of further studies have also shown that:

- the stimulants contained in chocolate
30 (theobromine, caffeine, tyramine and phenylethylamine) provide the body with an energy lift
- tryptophan, an essential amino acid, lessens anxiety and encourages the brain to
35 produce the neurotransmitter, serotonin
- chocolate encourages the body to release endorphins, the body's natural opiates, which can instil feelings of pleasure and reduce sensitivity to pain
40 - chocolate contains anandamide, another neurotransmitter, which acts like a cannabinoid to promote relaxation
- chocolate is a natural analgesic.

This all seems to be great news for the
45 chocolate lover. However, doctors have stressed that this report should not be viewed as confirmation that we can all eat as much of it as we can find! As with all food types, they advise us to enjoy the benefits of chocolate in
50 moderation.

Many of the same comprehension skills that are tested against one text are also tested with multiple texts. In particular, you will need to draw on your analysis and logic skills when answering questions related to multiple texts. When comparing a group of extracts, an examiner will also be looking for proof that you can:

- *read and understand a wide variety of material in a short period of time*
- *collate key information from more than one source*
- *compare different styles of writing and text formats*
- *understand how different formats can show different bias.*

a Extract placement

These questions are one example of a comparative type that tests your reasoning skills. Here is an example based on the given set of extracts:

> **1** Why do you think the extract entitled 'It's official – Chocolate is good for us!' has been placed at the end of the reading material? [4]

In this type of question you may think at first that you just need to refer to the named text, as the other sources are not mentioned specifically. Remember that all of the extracts have been selected and presented as a pack, so unless a question states that you should only look at one source, consider how all of them could contribute to an answer.

One of the best ways to compare a set of sources is to note down some key descriptors about each one. A visual format is often easier and quicker to read, so try jotting notes down in a grid or a spider diagram. For this example, a brief diagram for each text might look like this:

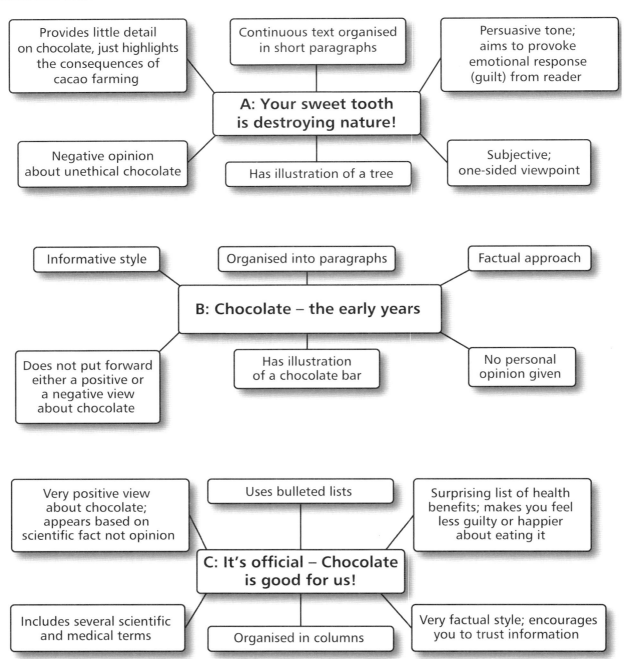

After comparing these three diagrams you should have a clearer picture of the content and style of all three extracts. You can now use these points to answer the question. For example:

Extract C is the most positive text about chocolate. It discusses scientific research rather than opinion, so it makes you feel that you can trust the information it offers. As a result, it leaves the reader in a positive, guilt-free frame of mind about eating chocolate.

Placing it at the end of the pack of reading material therefore helps to balance the negativity and feelings of guilt that the reader gets after reading the first extract. If Extract C was placed first, this balance would not be kept. If it had not been included in the selection at all, no positive benefits or points would have been made about chocolate.

b) Extract context

This type of question requires you to look not only at the content of each text, but also at the style in which they are presented. Here is a typical example based on the same set of extracts.

> **2** Each extract has come from a different type of source. Which of the extracts is most likely to have been taken from a textbook? Explain your answer. [4]

Following a step-by-step strategy is one of the best ways to make sure you consider all the relevant factors, in order to choose the right extract.

1. First think about the style you are being asked to look at, what it looks like, the language it uses, the writing style and so on. Writing a correct option checklist could provide useful ideas (see below).

2. Next, consider the format of each extract, reread the notes in the spider diagrams and compare them with your checklist. Which extract fits best with the checklist?

3. Then use your observations to develop an answer.

Using this approach, you could work through question 2 like this:

1. You are being asked to think here about how information in textbooks is written. A textbook is a form of explanatory text. Information in explanatory texts is usually written:

- in a factual, educational style
- without bias or personal opinion
- using full sentences and paragraphs
- in Standard English
- with keywords highlighted.

> **! Top Tip**
>
> For a more detailed reminder about the common features of different text types, see the 'Recognise different text types' section, pages 27–38.

2. It is easy to compare texts against a correct option checklist by drawing a quick grid:

Checklist	A	B	C
written in a factual, educational style	✗	✓	✓
includes no bias or personal opinion	✗	✓	✗
written in full sentences and paragraphs	✓	✓	✗
written in Standard English	✓	✓	✓
contains highlighted keywords	✗	✓	✗

3 So, in the case of this example it is possible to conclude that:

Extract B is likely to have been taken from a textbook because it has an informative and factual writing style. The text is written in Standard English, in full sentences and paragraphs, and has two key terms highlighted in bold. It also presents information about the history of chocolate without offering the writer's own opinion or including any bias. Readers are therefore not encouraged to think positively or negatively about chocolate: they are just being given facts.

This is not the case in Extracts A and C. In Extract A the reader is presented with a very negative view of chocolate and encouraged to feel guilty about eating unethical chocolate. In Extract C, the writer shows a more positive bias, listing many health benefits of chocolate and encouraging the reader to enjoy it.

Extract selection

You may be asked questions about the selection of extracts and how they relate to each other. Here is a typical example of this type of question:

> **3** Why do you think this reading material contains information about the early history of chocolate, as well as its related ecological effects and health benefits?

Again, the answer to this type of question requires you to consider all of the extracts. Refer back to the notes written in the spider diagrams drawn earlier. How does 'Chocolate – the early years' contrast with the other two extracts?

First, take each spider diagram in turn. How would you describe the aim of each text?

Extract A presents a clearly negative view of the way in which some chocolate is produced. It is written in a very strong, persuasive style because it is trying to scare the reader and make them feel guilty. It aims to convince the reader to change the type of chocolate they eat by highlighting the ecological effects caused by the way some chocolate is produced.

Extract B provides some detailed, factual information about the history of chocolate. It does not include any personal opinion or bias, so it is a more neutral account of chocolate production. Its aim is to inform and educate the reader about how the chocolate industry came to England.

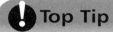

Top Tip

Don't forget that every extract you are given has a role to play. When comparing each extract, remember to comment on all of them, either by referring specifically to each extract or by summarising the information and style that they each offer.

Extract C offers a very positive view of chocolate. It lists the health benefits of chocolate, indicated by the results of recent research studies. Its aim is to present a different view from the traditional negative opinion that chocolate is bad for us.

Now, think about how these texts compare and why they have all been included in the pack. This should lead you to a logical answer. For example:

The three texts work together to inform, warn, entertain, explain and reassure the reader. Between them, they provide a brief history of chocolate, information about the effects of chocolate production and the positive health benefits that chocolate can have. Taken together, these extracts provide a complete, balanced pack of reading material about chocolate.

If Extract B was not included, the reader would not be presented with such a rounded or balanced view of the subject. The reader would also not learn anything about how the chocolate industry started in England.

Now it's your turn!

Read the three extracts below and then write the answers to the following comparative questions in your notebook. Ask someone to mark your responses when you have finished.

A

Liverpool Lime Street	Crewe	London Euston
6:30	7:00	8:00
7:30	8:00	9:00
8:30	9:00	10:00
9:30	10:00	11:00
10:30	11:00	12:00
11:30	12:00	13:00

B

Commuter joy for new express

Commuters were delighted last night as details of the new express from Liverpool Lime Street to London Euston were released.

The new express service will take passengers from Liverpool to London in an hour and a half with all of the luxury of first class made available for everyone. All seats have an inbuilt music and cinema system, there is wireless hi-fi for everyone and there are computer workstations in every carriage.

The buffet car includes a variety of delicious meals and fine wines with complimentary hot beverages served throughout the day.

The need for improved public transport has been created by increasing petrol prices, car emissions, road congestion and urban house prices. A spokesperson from Network North Rail said, "This service will mirror our Manchester to London express service, which has been tremendously popular. We might be a new company but our reputation is growing all the time. We have invested heavily in the new train stock but each engine is state-of-the-art and available for all. Our latest plan involves a cross-country express route, so expect an announcement in early 2009."

B Three steps to comprehension

C 3 Chicken, chicken, truth or dare

"You chicken or what?" sneered Ben. His group of five all flapped their arms and clucked loudly.

Jason could feel the anger bubble up inside of him. This time something snapped. He
5 would show them that he wasn't stupid, that he wasn't chicken. He pushed his hands deep into his pockets and crossed the yellow warning line. All he had to do was cross to the other side. How difficult could that be?

The light was green and everything was quiet. He jumped down onto the line, making sure he avoided anything live. He checked his watch; he had less than three minutes to cross to
10 the other side. "That's plenty of time," he thought. He had just placed his right foot over the next rail when he heard a faint rumbling in the distance. It couldn't be, could it?

His hands felt wet and clammy and he started to panic. Ben's group heard it too. The 3 o'clock was early! They started to back away from the track and Jason tried to follow as fast as he could. He moved his left foot quickly. A little too quickly ...

---

1 Why do you think a train timetable has been included? Explain your answer. `4`

2 Why do you think the excerpt from 'Chicken, chicken, truth or dare' has been placed at the end of this reading material? `4`

3 Each extract has come from a different type of source. Where do you think Extract B has been taken from? Explain your answer. `6`

✓ Parent Tip

When you read fiction or factual information, try to engage your child with their opinion. Asking them what they think and why is more productive than asking a closed yes or no question because it encourages your child to articulate their reasons rather than simply agree or disagree.

---

3 Evaluate your work

So far we have looked closely at how to understand and recognise a text as well as how to approach a range of different questions. The strategies you have learned along the way have also shown you the sort of elements you need to include in your responses in order to give full answers.

But are you still unsure about how you can check that what you are writing is correct and will be worth maximum marks? Don't worry. In the following pages you will find some useful checklists, summarising what you need to think about in order to make sure you write a good answer, as well as the key points that will help you avoid losing marks through carelessness. You will also be shown: how to recognise good, average and weak answers so that you can assess your own responses; how important checking your work can be and a useful technique for assessing your speed.

Write a good answer

Before you write, use your **HEART**:

- **H**ighlight the keywords and annotate your text – save time and be prepared.
- **E**arn maximum marks by focusing on the task – every second is precious.
- **A**ctively read the text – think about your ten key questions.
- **R**ead through a question more than once – make sure you know what you have to do.
- **T**ry to work out the meaning of unfamiliar words.

While you write, use your **FINGERS**:

- **F**it your answer to the marks per question – don't spend ages on one-point questions.
- **I**dentify where you can gain maximum marks – spend longer on these questions.
- **N**otes, diagrams and plans – structure your response and don't forget important points.
- **G**rammar, spelling, punctuation, handwriting – help the examiner to read and understand your answers.
- **E**rrors can be quickly dealt with – a neat, simple, crossed-out line is best.
- **R**emember the question – are you being asked to quote, give two sides, your opinion?
- **S**imple, precise answers – waffle takes up time and won't get you any extra marks.

After you write, use your **BRAIN**:

- **B**e ruthless – if an answer isn't good enough for you, it won't be for an examiner.
- **R**emember to attempt every question – guesses are better than blanks, so have a go.
- **A**ssess your answers – do they answer every part of the question? do they give enough information?
- **I**dentify incorrect spellings, grammar, punctuation – put it right and gain more marks.
- **N**ever be scared to make changes – examiners like proofreaders – but label changes clearly.

Avoid losing marks

This five-finger checklist makes it easy to see how you can avoid losing marks:

> **! Top Tip**
>
> If you struggle with time, complete the longer questions first to gain most marks, leaving the one-mark questions until last.

- Don't jump straight into the questions before reading the text fully.
- Don't rush through any question – plan your timing.
- Don't ramble or lose focus.
- Don't leave blanks – a guess is better than nothing.
- Don't use slang or colloquial language unless a question asks for it or a text includes it.

(B) Three steps to comprehension

By reading the text or texts fully before you attempt any question you can reduce the possibility of misunderstanding something. By planning your time, you can avoid having to rush any questions that might be worth several marks. By keeping focused, you can avoid lost marks through rambling. By making an educated guess instead of leaving a blank, you will give yourself the chance to gain another mark. Finally, by remembering to write in Standard English as a general rule, you will express yourself in the best possible way.

Assess your own answers

It is very important that you are able to assess your own answers and work out whether you have written a good, average or weak answer for any question.

Before we look at some examples of each level of question, try the following exercise.

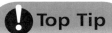

Top Tip

If you find yourself panicking in an exam or have a block when you cannot think straight, try this simple technique to help you refocus. Close your eyes and run through the alphabet in your mind, first in capital letters and then in lower-case letters. By making yourself concentrate on a simple, repetitive task like this, you will give your body and mind a chance to recover.

Now it's your turn!

Allow yourself 40 minutes to complete all ten comprehension questions. The scorebox at the end of each question shows the maximum marks available per question. **Before you have your paper marked, read through the section that follows the test.**

The Silver Unicorn

Once upon a time there existed the wild woods that covered the country with tall, towering trees. In those days, there were not many people, and those who existed lived in small settlements. They needed the forests for their survival. They would
5 hunt for animals and birds and pick fruit and berries from the trees.

Sylvac and his sister Vishnie lived in the Northern settlement and would often play in the woods trying to find animal footprints or birds' nests high up in the trees. They had heard that a beautiful unicorn lived in the woods, but they had never seen it. They had seen deer, wild boar, bears and wolves, but no unicorns.

10 One frosty winter morning, Sylvac and Vishnie set off into the woods as usual, when they heard an eerie sound. A woodpecker often made tapping noises on the tree trunks and stags could be heard ripping the velvet from their fierce antlers, but this was a very different noise. This was tip-tap-tip; far deeper than a woodpecker and duller than a stag. What on earth was it? Sylvac and Vishnie

15 moved quietly through the undergrowth, taking care to avoid standing on the newly fallen, rustling leaves and dry branches. Suddenly Vishnie stopped. Putting her finger up to her lips she signalled Sylvac to stand still and look ahead.

Just ahead of them the two children could see a body unlike anything else they had ever seen. A bent neck hid the head of the beast but then up it snapped, and

20   Sylvac and Vishnie saw a most astonishing sight. Upon its horse's head glowed a silver horn. Like some ghostly phantom, the creature was a pale, lunar white. The silver unicorn! The creature had not heard the two children and continued as before, making the strangest of noises. Putting its head down, the creature began head-butting a tree, trying hard to splinter off strips of bark. What was it trying to do?

25   Sylvac moved forward slowly with Vishnie tentatively following. Eventually they could see that the creature was feeding. By tearing the bark, it was exposing the sticky, yellow tree sap, which it lapped up slowly. Every time the creature licked the tree the children heard it whimper a little; Vishnie could tell that something was wrong. At that moment, Sylvac edged closer. Crack! He had stood
30   on a dry branch that went off like a gunshot.

1 Give another word for each of these five words as they are used in the context of the extract.

a usual (*line 10*) _____   **d** phantom (*line 21*) _____

b rustling (*line 16*) _____   **e** whimper (*line 28*) _____

c astonishing (*line 20*) _____

2 How did the children first know that the unicorn was there? Support your answer with evidence from the text.

_____

_____

_____

3 Explain in your own words what is meant by 'Vishnie tentatively following'.

_____

_____

_____

4 Underline one of these words which, as used in the passage, means the same as 'peel'.

   eerie   fierce   dry   lunar   splinter

5 Why do you think that Vishnie put her finger up to her lips?

_____

_____

6 Look again at the fourth paragraph. How does the author make the passage seem magical and full of mystery? Quote from the passage and explain your answer.

_____

_____

B) Three steps to comprehension

7 What style of writing is this and how do you know?

8 What time of the year is the story set and how do you know?

9 The word 'quietly' on line 15 is an adverb. Underline the word below which is not an adverb.

silently   tentatively   dreary   quickly

10 Continue the story from the end of the passage, showing what happens next. Write no more than 150 words.

END OF TEST

How did you find the exercise? Do you have a sense of how you have done?

The following section shows sample answers to the test you have just taken from three different pupils and the examiner's comments about their responses.

Pupil A achieved 15% on the test.

Pupil B gained 50% of the available marks.

Pupil C obtained a very high score of 94%.

Comparing the three answers and examiner's feedback for every question will help you to see what type of response each question required and show you where marks were gained or lost. As you read through these sample answers, think about the response you gave to each question. How do yours compare?

> **1** Give another word for each of these five words as they are used in the context of the extract.
>
> a usual (*line 10*) _____   d phantom (*line 21*) _____
>
> b rustling (*line 16*) _____   e whimper (*line 28*) _____
>
> c astonishing (*line 20*) _____
>
> 5

	Pupil A		Pupil B		Pupil C	
a	plain	✗	normal	✓	normal	✓
b	rotting	✗	crackling	✓	crunching	✓
c	surprising	✓	incredible	✓	amazing	✓
d	ghost	✗	ghost	✗	spirit	✓
e	laugh	✗	?	✗	wine	✗

Examiner's comments

Pupil A has only scored 1 mark on this question. He or she may not have read the context of each word carefully in order to give the correct answers, or may have a limited vocabulary and knowledge of words.

- 'Plain' can mean 'usual' but it doesn't make sense in the context used here.
- 'Rotting' is not a synonym for 'rustling'.
- 'Ghost' is a synonym for 'phantom' but it is not a good choice here because a 'ghostly ghost' is an odd phrase.
- 'Laugh' is not a synonym for 'whimper'.

Pupil B has scored 3 marks on this question. He or she has understood the meaning of four of the given words, showing good word knowledge, but needs to look more closely at context within sentences. The fifth word was not attempted so no mark can be awarded here.

- 'Ghost' is a synonym for 'phantom' but it is not a good choice here because a 'ghostly ghost' is an odd phrase.

Pupil C has scored 4 out of the 5 available marks. The fifth mark has not been given because an incorrect spelling has been used. However, this shows that he or she has fully understood the context in which each word has been used in the text, has good knowledge of word meanings and a wide vocabulary.

- Incorrect spelling of 'whine'.

2 How did the children first know that the unicorn was there? Support your answer with evidence from the text.

Pupil A	Pupil B	Pupil C
They saw it when they went into the woods. [0]	They heard it. [1]	The children first heard a strange noise that was deeper than a woodpecker and duller than a stag. They followed the noise until they reached the unicorn. [2]

Examiner's comments

Pupil A can be given no marks here. The children *first* heard a noise, *then* they saw the unicorn. Pupil A needs to make sure he or she reads all question instructions carefully.

Pupil B's answer has only been awarded one mark, because it is not supported by any evidence from the text. Pupil B has forgotten to check whether he or she has answered the question fully.

Pupil C has been awarded the full two marks because the correct answer has been given and it includes the relevant information from the text.

3 Explain in your own words what is meant by 'Vishnie tentatively following'

Pupil A	Pupil B	Pupil C
She happily followed. [0]	Vishnie was unsure about where they were going and hesitated as she walked. [1]	Vishnie carefully and cautiously followed Sylvac because she didn't want to tread on leaves or branches that would make a noise in case this startled the creature. [2]

Examiner's comments

Pupil A can be given no marks because the meaning of 'tentatively' is incorrect. This again shows that Pupil A may have a more limited vocabulary than Pupils B and C.

Pupil B has been given only one mark. Pupil B is showing that he or she has a general understanding of the term 'tentatively', but does not give a clear enough explanation in the context of the extract.

Pupil C has been awarded full marks. The phrase 'carefully and cautiously' is a good description of the word 'tentatively' and the explanation that follows shows a clear understanding of the context.

> 4 Underline one of these words which, as used in the passage, means the same as 'peel'.
>
>   eerie   fierce   dry   lunar   splinter   [1]

Pupil A	Pupil B	Pupil C
lunar [0]	lunar [0]	splinter [2]

Examiner's comments

Pupil A receives no mark because this is the incorrect option. If Pupil A had replaced each word as it is used in the text with the given word, the most sensible answer should have become clear. However, if he or she was unfamiliar with any of the words in the question, it was better to guess than to leave a blank.

Pupil B receives no mark because this is the incorrect option.

Pupil C has selected the correct option. In the context of this extract, the word 'splinter' is used to show that the unicorn was trying to peel off strips of bark.

> 5 Why do you think that Vishnie put her finger up to her lips?   [1]

Pupil A	Pupil B	Pupil C
She was scared and going to bite her nails. [0]	Because she had seen the unicorn. [0]	Vishnie uses this signal to tell Sylvac to be quiet. She had seen the unicorn ahead of them and didn't want to scare it away. [1]

Examiner's comments

Pupil A cannot be given a mark here because he or she has misunderstood the meaning behind Vishnie's action. The clues in the text, such as 'Sylvac and Vishnie moved quietly…' and '… she signalled Sylvac to stand still…' have been missed.

Pupil B cannot be awarded a mark here. This statement does not explain Vishnie's action in enough detail to fully answer the question.

Pupil C has given an excellent answer that clearly explains the reason behind Vishnie's action and uses the word 'signal', which is taken from the text.

> 6 Look again at the fourth paragraph. How does the author make the passage seem magical and full of mystery? Quote from the passage and explain your answer.   [8]

Pupil A	Pupil B	Pupil C
The author says a most astonishing sight. And the creature had not heard the two children and continued as before, making the strangest of noises. [1]	This passage seems magical because it is describing the unicorn. The writer says it has a horn that glows and that it looks like a ghostley phantom. It is silver and is making strange noises. [4]	The author describes the creature as being 'unlike anything they had ever seen' but doesn't tell us what it is straight away. Insted, the writer uses words such as 'beast' and 'astonishing' to help emfasise the mystery. This is emfasised more by the description of the unicorn's silver horn, and the word 'glowing' makes it sound magical. The 'ghostly phantom' is another magical phrase and 'pale, lunar white' makes the beast seem more ghostlike. The creature is unlike any other horse and it is making 'the strangest of noises'. We are told that it is headbutting a tree but we don't know why yet. It is a strange thing for an animal to do, which also suggests a mysterious nature. [7]

Examiner's comments

Pupil A has taken two quotations from the right paragraph but has not explained these sufficiently to answer the question fully. This response can therefore only be awarded one point.

Pupil B has shown more understanding of the passage. He or she has picked out some of the words and phrases that describe the unicorn but has not fully shown why these terms make the passage appear full of mystery. The word 'ghostly', which has been taken from the passage, has also been spelt incorrectly. Only half of the marks can be given for this answer.

Pupil C's answer is very detailed and remains focused on the question. It refers to the terms 'magical', 'mystery' and 'mysterious' taken from the question and includes all of the keywords from the passage. This answer highlights that this pupil understands the passage and the literary features that shape the text. Pupil C shows good knowledge of grammar and spelling here. As there are two spelling mistakes ('inste**a**d' and 'em**ph**asise', which appears twice), one mark has been deducted.

7 What style of writing is this and how do you know? [2]

Pupil A	Pupil B	Pupil C
This is from a book because there are characters called Sylvac and Vishnie and they go into the woods and find a silver unicorn. [0]	This passage is from a fairy story because it is about a unicorn. [1]	The piece opens with 'Once upon a time', which is like the beginning of a fairy story. The writing is prose and, because it is about a silver unicorn, a piece of fiction. There is a clear narrator and the story has characters. I think it is from an adventure story about magical creatures. [2]

The secrets of Comprehension

Examiner's comments

Pupil A has recognised that the extract includes details of characters, but this feature does not identify the style of writing. No firm conclusions are drawn, for example, about whether the extract is fiction or fact, and repeating the storyline strays away from the question. No marks can be given, because this response does not answer the question.

Pupil B has correctly noted that this passage reads as if it might be from a fairy story because it mentions a unicorn. However, to be given full marks, this answer needs to be more detailed and include other clues found in the text.

Pupil C has followed the same logical thought process as Pupil B (the passage must be fiction because unicorns are not real). However, this conclusion is further supported here with reference to additional clues in the text (the presence of the narrator for example). The answer also shows a clear understanding of writing style (the opening phrase is often found in fairy stories) and it offers an opinion on where this extract may have come from. This carefully thought-out answer is worth full marks.

8 What time of the year is the story set and how do you know? [2]

Pupil A	Pupil B	Pupil C
Don't know. [0]	This story is set in autumn. [1]	The text says that there are 'newly fallen rustling leaves and dry branches' so it must be autumn time because this is when the leaves fall from trees and branches can break off. [2]

Examiner's comments

Pupil A has not attempted to answer this question. The clues about the season that are given in the text have been missed and no guess has been made, so no marks can be given here.

Pupil B has only answered the first part of the question here. Pupil B has not supported this statement with evidence from the text, so only one mark can be awarded.

Pupil C has given an accurate answer that is supported with a relevant quotation from the text. This is worth full marks.

9 The word 'quietly' on line 15 is an adverb. Underline the word below which is not an adverb.

    silently   tentatively   dreary   quickly

Pupil A	Pupil B	Pupil C
tentatively [0]	dreary [1]	dreary [1]

Examiner's comments

Pupil A may have misread the question here, or could be unsure about how to form different parts of speech. If Pupil A had worked through each option, asking 'Is it possible to walk silently/tentatively/dreary/quickly?', the correct option would have been easier to identify.

Pupil B has chosen the correct option.

Pupil C has chosen the correct option.

10 Continue the story from the end of the passage, showing what happens next. Write no more than 150 words.

Pupil A	Pupil B	Pupil C
So the silver unicorn ran away because he was scared and then sylvac and vishny went home and then they told there mum and dad about it and then it meant they had seen the silver unicorn but they didn't never see it again. [2]	The noise was so deafning that the unicorn jumped and looked straight at Vishnie and Sylvac with its big, mysterious eyes. It stared at them for a moment or two and then turned and darted off deep into the woods. "Let's follow it and see where it goes," said Sylvac. "OK," said Vishnie. And that was the last anyone saw of the children. [5]	The creature's head snapped up straight and it looked around frantically. Vishnie and Sylvac held their breath, praying that the creature would not be afraid, but it was too late. As soon as the beast turned it's frightened eyes towards the two children, it let out a long, low moan, flicked back it's silvery mane and galloped away. "Quick!" shouted Sylvac, "Let's follow him!" but the creature had already disappeared. Vishnie ran over to the tree and touched the splintered bark. "Look Sylvac!" she called. The trace of the unicorn's silvery tongue was slowly evaporating, with tiny particles of magical dust settling into the sticky tree sap. "We must come back tomorrow to see if he returns, Sylvac," sighed Vishnie. "Something is wrong and we must try to help." Sylvac agreed. The following day they returned to the same spot and waited... [10]

Examiner's comments

Pupil A has received only two marks for this answer because it follows the basic line of the story but has not included much additional detail. It also shows that Pupil A has limited knowledge of punctuation, spelling and grammar. The final part of the story has been written in one sentence; names have been written without capital letters; the wrong spelling of 'there' and Vishnie have been used and the sentence ends with a double negative.

Pupil B has begun to think creatively here while following the plot line of the extract. Some basic dialogue is introduced and a few elements of more advanced vocabulary have been used (deafening, mysterious, darted). This answer shows an average level of spelling ('deafening' has been spelt incorrectly), punctuation and grammar, but the writing does not really follow the style of the original text. This new plot line is not developed in very much detail, is short and ends abruptly. Only half marks can be awarded for this continuation of the story.

Pupil C has achieved full marks because this is an imaginative ending that follows on closely from the original text. This effect is created by using phrases from the extract (the creature's head 'snapped up', the 'splintered bark', the 'sticky tree sap'), and by using a similar writing style. The mention of 'magical dust' retains the fairy story theme, and the sense of mystery is continued in the final sentence where the reader is left to guess what will happen next. Generally, Pupil C demonstrates excellent spelling skills (except for the misuse, on two occasions, of the apostrophe in 'its'), uses accurate punctuation for dialogue and narrative and includes some interesting vocabulary (galloped, silvery tongue, evaporating, particles and a range of synonyms for 'said'). The length of this piece of writing has also been judged very carefully because it is just within the word limit.

Here are the examiner's final comments about how each pupil performed on the test and some tips for how they could improve their comprehension skills.

Pupil	Score out of 34	%	Examiner's summary
A	4	15	Most of the questions were attempted but answers rarely fulfilled all of the question requirements. Answers were often too short, lacked detailed explanation, didn't include quotes from the text or were misunderstood. Poor spellings, word knowledge and grammar use also caused Pupil A to lose marks. This pupil needs to focus closely on improving: spelling skills, breadth of vocabulary, grammar and punctuation knowledge. More practice at comprehension tests, using a range of text types, lengths and so on, is also needed to help improve performance.
B	17	50	Responses show a moderate ability in comprehension, a general understanding of spelling, grammar and punctuation and average word knowledge. To avoid losing marks through careless mistakes, Pupil B should focus on improving core comprehension skills such as: reading the question carefully; writing detailed and focused responses; and using quotes from the text to support answers. Spelling, grammar and punctuation skills should be reinforced and word knowledge could also be expanded to allow responses to be developed further.
C	33	97	This high mark reflects strong comprehension skills. Responses show that this pupil has the ability to: read and understand the requirements of a question; write purposeful responses that remain focused on the question; read a text and then use it to support answers; write creatively and follow a given writing style. This pupil's excellent spelling and grammatical skills, wide vocabulary and word knowledge are also noticeable throughout all answers. To maintain this sound skills base, Pupil C should continue to: practise a range of comprehension exercises; read widely to support vocabulary knowledge; and look back over spelling, grammar and punctuation rules.

Now you have read through this section, ask an adult to mark your paper against the answers given here. Talk through any questions where you lost marks and look back at the examiner's comments for useful hints about what a full answer to each question required. What might the examiner have said about your answers? Were your answers closest to Pupil A, B or C? Reread the relevant examiner's summary for ideas on how you could improve.

● Check your work

As you saw from some of Pupil A and Pupil B's responses in the last exercise, marks are often lost through carelessness and misunderstanding rather than lack of knowledge. However, many of these errors can be avoided if you leave enough time to check your work.

It is important that you understand how to check your work actively because in an exam no one else can check for you. Have another look at the 'Write a good answer' and 'Avoid losing marks' checklists (pages 85 and 86) to remind yourself what to look out for during the checking process. One other vital question to ask yourself at this stage is:

Have I seen every question?

Make sure you turn every page over; there may be questions on the other side that you have missed!

> Now it's your turn!
>
> Below is a short comprehension exercise worth 15 marks. A child has sat the paper and you are the examiner. Before you read the extract and mark the paper, look at the questions that were set (see below) and then answer the following questions.

1 What is on the tree to decorate it? [4]

2 What month of the year do you think it is and why? [2]

3 What colour do you think cranberry is? [1]

4 What do you think 'a light sprinkling of tinsel reflected each light a thousand times' means? [2]

5 What do you think these words mean as used in the text? [6]

    a abundance   **b** surreptitious   **c** bedecked

- *How many items do you think should be listed in the answer to question 1?* _____
- *How many parts are there to question 2?* _____
- *Will question 3 require a paragraph answer?* _____
- *Will the answer to question 4 require a detailed explanation?* _____
- *Should the answers to question 5 refer to the text?* _____

Here is the completed paper. Read the extract and then allocate a mark to each of the following answers. The pupil finished the paper within the time frame but did not use the last few minutes to check any answers. Keep the checklists (see pages 85 and 86) and your answers to the five questions above in mind as you read through and mark each response.

Read this extract, then answer the following questions.

> The tree was huge and took up nearly a third of the floor area. The settee had to be pushed into the corner and even then, the television could not be fully seen without baubles and branches getting in the way, but nobody cared. It was the most beautiful tree they had ever had. Christine and Nick had decorated it all afternoon with baubles made of glass or silk in rich shades of cranberry, gold and silver. Glowing fairy lights twinkled in abundance and a light sprinkling of tinsel reflected each light a thousand times.
>
> Beneath the tree an enormous pile of presents grew. Big parcels, little packages, perfect boxes and funny shapes were all bedecked with bows, ribbons and stars. Christine could hardly wait to find out which ones were for her, but Mum had strictly forbidden any shaking, sniffing or surreptitious peeping at any gift.
>
> Nick held a chair as Christine climbed up to place some festive stickers on the window. "There!" she said, looking with satisfaction at her handiwork, "Now Santa will know where to stop." Nick agreed, and together they raced into the kitchen to see if Mum needed any more help.

1 What is on the tree to decorate it?

baubles, fairy lights and tinsel ⎕ 4

2 What month of the year do you think it is and why?

It is Christmas time. ⎕ 2

3 What colour do you think cranberry is?

Cranberries must be red because I drink cranberry juice and that is red. ⎕ 1

4 What do you think 'a light sprinkling of tinsel reflected each light a thousand times' means?

Tinsel is shiny and it sometimes looks like a mirror. This means that the lights were reflected in the tinsel, as if there were lots of lights on the tree. ⎕ 2

5 What do you think these words mean as used in the text?

a abundance

Don't know.

> **b** surreptitious
>
> Mum wouldn't let Nick and Christine go near the presents so they couldn't shake, sniff or secretly peep at them. Surreptitious means sneaky or secretive.
>
> **c** bedecked
>
> If something is bedecked with bows and ribbons it is decorated with them.
>
> | 6 |
>
> END OF TEST
>
> | 15 TOTAL |

How did you get on marking the paper? Add the marks up that you have given and write the total in the box. Did you think of any comments as you scored the answers? Note down your thoughts here.

Now compare your marks with the examiner's scoring and read the examiner's feedback below. Did you notice the same things as you marked the paper?

Question number	Question score	Examiner's comments
1	3	Only 3 marks can be given here because two types of bauble were mentioned in the text (glass baubles and silk baubles) but they were not listed separately in the answer. A mark has been carelessly lost here, which might have been avoided if the answer had been checked.
2	0	This is a two-part question that asks for a month of the year and evidence from the text. It must be December because the text mentions decorating a tree, presents and Santa. No marks can be given here because Christmas is not a month and no reference to the text is made in the answer. It is clear from the pupil's answer that they have understood the text is about Christmas. Both of these lost marks could have been retrieved if the question and answer had been checked.
3	1	Red is correct but only a one-word answer was required.
4	2	This answer is worth both marks because it gives a full explanation of what is meant by the phrase in the text.

The secrets of Comprehension

Question number	Question score	Examiner's comments
5a	0	No marks can be given here because the question has not been attempted. It would have been better to guess at the meaning of this unfamiliar word than to leave a blank space.
5b	2	This answer is worth both marks because it gives a full explanation of the word in the context of the text.
5c	2	This answer is worth both marks because it gives a good explanation of the word in the context of the text.
TOTAL	10/15	

So how did you do? Did you think of the same or similar comments to the examiner's feedback above? This pupil could have gained at least three more marks if he or she had checked his or her answers. This exercise shows just how vital it is to check your responses against each question!

● Assess your speed

You should always try to complete a test a few minutes before the time is up so you can check your work. However, it can be difficult to estimate how quickly you need to work through a paper to ensure you complete all the questions, while still leaving enough time at the end to check over what you have written.

Try following the practice technique outlined below. It will help you gauge the speed at which you need to work through comprehension tests in order to make sure there is time to assess your answers. The same technique can be used for a comprehension test of any length.

You may find it helpful to start with a short comprehension exercise (perhaps lasting 15 minutes) and work up to longer papers (lasting 50 minutes to an hour, for example), so you can develop your comprehension and timing skills more steadily.

Before you start:

1. First, make sure you have a quiet, well-lit place to sit. If you need to have a drink or to use the toilet, now is the time, before your test begins.

2. Then, check that everyone knows you are going to work through a timed test paper, so that you are not interrupted part way through!

3. Next, place your watch or a clock nearby so you can keep an eye on the time. It's a good idea to use an alarm clock so that you can set it to ring when half of the time has gone, when there are only five minutes to go and again when your time is up.

4. Finally, you may prefer to ask someone to give you some time-checks as you work – perhaps when you have had half the time, when there are only five minutes left and when your time is up.

Here is a useful method for working out your 'natural' working time as you work through your first test paper:

- *Note down your start time on the front of the paper.*
- *Quickly flick through the paper to check how many questions there are.*
- *Begin working through the questions as quickly and carefully as you can.*
- *At the halfway point, put a mark next to the question you have reached and carry on.*
- *At the 'five minutes from the end' point, put a small mark next to the question you have reached and carry on.*
- *When the time is up, stop and make a mark next to the last question you completed.*
- *If you haven't finished the paper in the time, check how far you were from the end.*

You now need to ask someone to mark your paper and discuss your answers with you. If you didn't finish the paper in time, think about which questions took you the longest time to answer. Think about the following points:

Top Tip

You may find it useful at this point to time how long it takes you to answer the rest of the questions, because this will tell you how much more time you would have needed to complete the paper.

- *Why did they take more time?*
- *Were they worth more than one mark?*
- *Do you need to revise a particular question type?*
- *Could you have used a different technique to find the answers more quickly?*

Once your first paper has been marked, make a chart so you can see your time progress through the paper. Here is a suggested model for the chart:

DATE:					
Paper number or title					
Time limit					
Number of questions completed at half time					
Number of questions completed at 5 minutes before end					
Total number of questions completed in time limit					
Marks achieved in time limit					
Number of questions not completed in time limit					
Number of extra minutes needed to complete paper					
Number of minutes checking time available at end of paper					

After a few days, remind yourself of your previous times so that you can aim to beat them in the next test. Set yourself another test of the same length and time limit and work through it using the same timing techniques. Record your results in the chart as before. After a few days' break, do another test in the same way, and so on. As you practise by recording your times, you should find that your speed of working will gradually increase and that you will be able to successfully pace yourself to allow time for checking before the end of a test.

> **Top Tip**
>
> This 'practice in time' technique works for any type of test, so you can try it with other subjects to make sure you have enough time to check your answers. Take care not to rush through a test paper just to ensure you have lots of checking time. If you have to go back and change most of your answers you'll end up running out of time!

> **Parent Tip**
>
> Create regular opportunities for your child to complete and record these timed practice sessions. They are one of the best ways for your child to see his or her progress. Remember to be available during each session for time-checks, marking and to give feedback on responses.

Final thoughts

I hope that you have found this book an informative and useful resource and that you will now have lots of ideas, techniques and strategies for performing well in comprehension tests.

Now is the ideal time to put your new skills into practice! Why not have a go at the comprehension test papers that accompany this book? (See the Bond web site and the central pull-out section for copies.) Once you have completed a test (and hopefully been able to check your answers in the time frame!), ask someone to mark the paper with you. You can then see what mark you would get if the paper was an actual exam.

If you find that you have lost marks anywhere, look back through the sections in this book to remind you of the techniques you need to practise and to help you see how you can improve next time.

There are also lots of other books that can help develop your overall literacy skills. These are listed in the Additional resources section of Appendix C on page 110 and are worth working through to strengthen any weak areas.

Whether you have used this book because you will be sitting a comprehension exam soon or just to help support your general English skills, I wish you all the best and every success for the future.

Michellejoy

C Appendices

1 Glossary

active – describes a phrase where someone or something is actually doing something

adjective – a word used to describe a noun

adverb – a word used to describe a verb

alliteration – repetition of sound patterns (*She* sells sea *sh*ells from the sea *sh*ore)

antonym – a word with an opposite meaning to another word

annotate – to write notes on something

caesura – a pause near the middle of a line of poetry

chronological – following the time sequence in which events actually occurred

collocation – a set of words that are often grouped together

compound word – two or more words put together to make a new idea

conjunction – a word used to connect two or more phrases

dialect – the style of language of a particular region

dialogue – a conversation between two or more characters

direct speech – the actual words people say to each other

elision – the omission of a sound or syllable in speech

enjambment – when a line of poetry runs into the next line without a pause

figurative – a style of writing that does not use words in their literal sense, but creates imagery through metaphor and simile

first person – the form of a verb that refers to the speaker, or a group including the speaker (I, we)

formal – following rules; official

homophone – a word that sounds the same as another but has a different meaning and is spelt differently

idiom – a phrase whose meaning cannot be worked out from the meaning of the individual words

imagery – language used to bring pictures into the reader's mind

imperative – a verb form that expresses a command or an order (Stop!)

informal – casual, relaxed

keyword – a significant word or phrase in a piece of text

literally – using words in their most basic sense, with no metaphors intended

metaphor – a word or phrase used with reference to something that it does not literally apply to, in order to create imagery

narrator – the storyteller

noun – a naming word (a person, object, group or date)

onomatopoeia – words that sound the same as their meanings (fizz, sploosh)

paragraph – a sentence or set of sentences describing one stage of a piece of writing, separated from the next paragraph by either a line space or an indent

paraphrase – to put a quotation into your own words

passive – describes a phrase where someone or something is having something done to them

personification – giving a human attribute to something non-human (the sun smiled)

phonetic – relating to speech sounds

prefix – a group of letters added to the front of a root word to change its meaning

preposition – a word that shows the position, direction or timing of a noun

pronoun – a word used instead of a noun (he, they, it)

prose – a piece of continuous writing

quote – repeat a phrase or passage from a text

quotation – a phrase or passage repeated from a text

recount – a retelling of an event or series of events

reported speech – what people say to each other, but not using their actual words

root, root word – the main part of a word to which prefixes and suffixes can be added

scenario – a situation or an event

script, playscript – the written form of a play

second person – the form of the verb that refers to the person being spoken to (you)

simile – a phrase that compares one thing with another using 'like' or 'as'

Standard English – a form of English that is seen as correct English

stanza – a group of lines that form a short unit in a poem, usually separated from the next stanza by a line space

strategy – a method of working out a problem

structure – the shape of a piece of writing and how it is organised

suffix – a group of letters added to the end of a root word to change its meaning

synonym – a word with a similar meaning to another word

tense – used to show whether a verb is in the past, present or future

third person – the form of the verb that refers to someone other than the speaker and the person being spoken to (Lucy, he, they)

verb – an action word that shows doing, having or being

vocabulary – the range of words that a person knows

2 Answers

Bold numbers in square brackets show mark allocations for multiple point questions. Terms in italics highlight possible answers, but answers may vary for these questions. Suggested marking schemes have been provided for questions requiring free text or personal opinion responses. Half marks should not be awarded.

1 Read and understand the text

Discover active reading test (pages 9–10)

1 Lucy – badgers [1]   Edmund – foxes [1]
  Susan – rabbits [1]   Peter – stags [1]
2 Susan
3 b [1] and d [1]
4 a [1] and c [1]
5 Answer should indicate that:
  - it was during the war [1]
  - the countryside was not under the same threat of air raids. [1]
6 Answer should refer to lines in the text that indicate that:
  - that the Professor had an odd appearance (lines 7–9) [1]
  - Lucy was the youngest child (line 10). [1]
7 a *wonderful, lovely, super* [1]
  b *relates to walking in a particular way – in an orderly line, like a troop of soldiers* [1]
8 [1] mark each for any five of these points (or similar); each point must refer to text:
  - He is the second youngest child. (lines 10–11)
  - He seems ill-mannered; he wants to laugh at the Professor. (line 11)
  - He is tired. (line 17)
  - He might be missing his mother; he accuses Susan of talking like their mother. (line 20)
  - He thinks he's a bit of a 'know-it-all'; his comment to Lucy about the noise. (line 30)
  - He seems to have a negative, miserable character; his reaction to the weather (line 41) and he is told to stop grumbling. (line 45)
9 [1] mark each for any five of these points (or similar):
  - excited or thrilled that this is an adventure
  - nervous or scared for Lucy and her safety
  - wondering or curious what will happen next
  - confused at the trees or snow in the wardrobe
  - disbelieving or suspicious because what is happening is impossible
  - questioning how this can happen
  - worried that Lucy is alone
  - annoyed or angry that Lucy has been left alone and not looked after
10 [1] mark each for any five of these points (or similar):
   The author may have chosen Lucy because she is the youngest child, so:
   - it will create more tension when she finds herself on her own
   - it is more of a surprise to the reader to see her have her own adventure
   - she is more likely to get lost in the house
   - the reader will associate more with her
   - the author wants to make her feel more important
   - the author wants to show that Lucy can be brave
   - the author wants to show that young girls can have adventures too.

Recognise different text types (practice activities)

Narrative texts (page 28)
[1] mark each for any five of these points:
- Evidence of a narrator in each – the writer or observer in 'A' as it is written in the third person; the writer or a character in 'B' as it is written in the first person.
- Evidence of plot in both.
- Both use descriptive language and suspense in writing style.
- Both extracts of continuous text.
- 'A' shows invented language: 'deathstar', 'astrogation monitor'.
- 'B' shows dialogue.

Poetry (page 29)
[1] mark each for any five of these points:
- Both follow rhyming patterns.
- Both have a clear rhythm.
- Both use short lines.
- Both consist of one stanza (are written in an unbroken column of text).
- Both use punctuation to create rhythm: 'A' has a comma in line 5 to give a pause; 'B' has no punctuation at the end of line 3 to create a run-on effect.
- 'A' uses sound effects: alliteration: 'Creation to Creator'; elision: 'ne'er'.
- 'A' uses archaic language: 'Thine', 'asunder'.
- 'B' includes humour.

Scripts (page 31)
[1] mark each for any five of these points:
- The content of both extracts consists mainly of dialogue.
- Both extracts start a new line when a different character speaks.

- Neither extract includes speech marks.
- Both extracts show stage directions in brackets.
- 'A' shows an example of the acts and scenes structure.
- 'B' includes a narrator who sets the scene before the characters speak.
- 'B' shows examples of phonetic language ('stayin', 'outta', 'yeah', 'gotta').

Explanatory texts (page 32)
[1] mark each for any five of these points:
- A keyword is clearly highlighted.
- Explains the topic clearly to the reader.
- Key points drawn out in a bulleted list.
- Well structured and draws a conclusion.
- Is written in an objective, formal style and without bias.
- Includes subject-specific terms.
- Includes navigational aids (heading, cross-reference link).

Recounts and reports (page 34)
[1] mark each for any five of these points:
- 'B' includes a graphic feature.
- Both are factual accounts.
- Both follow a clear structure.
- Both use subject-specific terms.
- 'A' is general in reference to 'the Romans'; 'B' is specific about 'The Railway Inn'.
- 'A' is in the third person; 'B' is in the first person.
- 'A' is an impersonal account; 'B' is a personal account.
- 'A' is non-chronological; 'B' is chronological.

Instructions (page 36)
[1] mark each for any five of these points:
- Both texts tell you how to do something.
- Both contain short sentences.
- Both use formal, direct, impersonal language.
- Both use imperatives.
- Both include subject-specific terms.
- 'B' uses time connectives.
- 'B' uses diagrams to illustrate steps.
- Both use lists (numbered and bulleted).

Letters (page 37)
[1] mark each for any five of these points:
- Both letters have the writer's address and date on the right-hand side.
- Both letters are signed.
- Both letters use the present tense and are written in the first person.
- 'A' uses an informal greeting; 'B' uses a formal greeting.
- 'A' uses an informal ending; 'B' uses a formal ending.
- 'A' has all content in one paragraph; 'B' structures content in separate paragraphs.
- 'B' includes the recipient's name and address details.

2 Understand the question

Reorganise and select information (pages 40–47)

1. b the Industrial Revolution – a period of growth following the invention of many mechanical processes
   c chain making – an industry that many women took part in
   d steel industry – the major industry during this time
   e waterways – used to transport cargo
2. b Family trees
   c any two of the following:
   - parish records
   - birth, marriage and death certificates from the General Records Office
   - the National Census
   - the Internet
   - the National War Graves Commission.
   d National Census
3. [1] mark for each correct pairing:

WORLD WAR I		WORLD WAR II	
BATTLE	COUNTRY	BATTLE	COUNTRY
Gallipoli	Turkey	El Alamein	North Africa
The Somme	France	Arnhem	Holland
Passchendaele	Belgium	Dunkirk	France

4. See text, page 44
5. d
6–7. c and f
8.
   - it provided a form of transport [1]
   - it provided a variety of jobs in manufacturing and processing [1]
   - the development of communities around the canals [1]
9. [1] mark for each of the following points:
   - finding parish records
   - ordering birth, marriage and death certificates
   - looking at the National Census
   - contacting the National War Graves Commission
   - Internet research

Apply word knowledge and grammar (pages 47–58)

1–3 noun: people or allotments [1]; pronoun: we [1]
4 See text, page 50
5 personification
6 a Either: 'Allotments originated in the eighteenth century…' or 'You would think that I lived in the middle of…'.
  b See text, page 51
  c 'In my allotment this year I will be growing…'
7 See text, pages 51–53
8 *productive, rich*
9 a See text, pages 54–55
  b manufacturing: *to make something, especially using factory machines to turn over a large number of items* [1]
  process: *a series of actions, methods or operations* [1]
10 'We all need to be aware of our carbon footprint' and [1] 'to reduce the amount of travel our food has' [1]
11 'As the allotment is at the bottom of my road'
12 a canning [1]; shopping [1]
  b If a word has a short vowel sound before the last letter [1], double the consonant before adding the suffix. [1]
13 a ration [1]
  b vary [1]
  c manufacture [1]
  d vital [1]

Find, deduce and infer information (pages 58–64)

1 See text, pages 60–61
2 [1] mark for each of these three points (or similar):
  Television advertising:
  - can reach many drivers at the same time, spreading the safety message rapidly
  - can show the effects of having a road accident at different speeds, having a greater impact on people's driving habits
  - can make pedestrians and cyclists more aware of road hazards.
3 See text, page 62
4 d
5 See text, pages 63–64
6 [1] mark each for any three of these points (or similar):
  A crossing patrol person:
  - is usually in the same place every day, so pedestrians and motorists are aware of the crossing area
  - holds a fluorescent 'lollipop' that is easily seen, so motorists can see it well ahead and start to slow down
  - is a responsible adult who can judge when it is safe to cross
  - is able to stop the traffic so people can cross the road safely.

Prepare a knowledge-based response (pages 65–69)

1 See text, page 67
2 Strings: *viola, harp* [1]
  Brass: *tuba, cornet* [1]
  Woodwind: *oboe, saxophone, recorder* [1]
  Percussion: *drums, triangle, bells* [1]
3 *United Kingdom* [1], *France* [1], *Spain* [1]
4 See text, pages 68–69
5 Italy shares a border with Germany. [1] This is why Germany is referred to as 'a neighbour'. [1]

Introduce personal opinion (pages 69–77)

practice activity (page 72)
- Two sensible reactions listed in diagram, such as *Solomon gets too upset to read the poem.* [2]
- One reaction described in a short paragraph. [2]

practice activity (page 74)
Use the sample answer on pages 73–74 and the marking scheme below to award marks:
- Up to [3] marks for writing a sensible ending that fits with the story so far.
- Up to [2] marks for following the same style as the extract (similar choice of words, similar length of sentences, same scene and characters and so on).
- [1] mark for writing within the word limit (130–150 words).
- [1] mark for correct grammar and punctuation (the correct use of tense, starting each sentence with a capital letter and so on).
- [1] mark for good overall spelling.

practice activity (page 77)
[1] mark for each of the following factors:
- Inclusion of at least two relevant facts about researching family history.
- Stating own viewpoint clearly.
- Including reference to the text as well as own knowledge.
- Discussing both sides of the argument.
- Organising ideas into a logical structure.
- Drawing ideas together into a summary or conclusion.
- Good grammar and punctuation (full sentences, capital letters and so on).
- Good overall spelling.

Compare texts (pages 77–84)

practice activity (page 83–84)
1.
   - A train timetable is an objective, unbiased piece of information. [1]
   - It provides facts and data only. [1]
   - This extract provides the balance between the positive view of trains found in 'B' [1] and the negative view given by 'C'. [1]
2.
   - 'C' provides a sober warning to the reader of the dangers of train lines. [1]
   - Being the last article, it leaves a lasting effect on the reader. [1]
   - If 'A' was last, it would leave the reader with no lasting reminder of the topic. [1]
   - If 'B' was last, the reader would be left feeling very positive about rail travel. [1]
3. A newspaper or magazine article. [1]
   [1] mark each for any five of these points:
   The extract:
   - is arranged in columns
   - has a slogan heading
   - is factual
   - includes external quotes
   - includes personal opinion and bias
   - is continuous text
   - has a clear paragraph structure
   - uses full sentences
   - is written in Standard English.

Graded test papers

Practice Test 1

1. d
2. adjective
3.
   - It was seen as a means of letting off steam (line 9). [1]
   - It encouraged a healthy, active lifestyle (line 10). [1]
4. a future   b past
5. A newspaper or magazine article. [1]
   [1] mark for any three of these points:
   The extract:
   - is arranged in columns
   - has a slogan heading
   - is factual
   - includes external quotes
   - is continuous text
   - has a clear paragraph structure
   - uses full sentences
   - is written in Standard English.
6. [1] mark each for any two of these points (or similar):
   - something that divides groups of people
   - separate groups with their own defined set of thoughts and ideas
   - a group of people opposed to or intolerant of another group's thoughts and ideas
   - a form of racism or prejudice.
7. a Show Racism the Red Card [1]
   b tackle racism in Scottish football [1]
   c more proactive in giving life bans to fans who show racial or religious hatred [1]
   d severe punishments for players who display any racial or religious intolerance [1]
8. a alliteration [1]   b idiom [1]
9. 'it's as if floodgates have opened' [1]; 'Hoards of spectators are spilling onto the pitch' [1]
10. a *chaos, madness* [1]   b *fight, disagreement* [1]
11. a metaphor
12. Whisky is a form of alcohol. [1] Alcohol is flammable. [1] Whisky causes fire to spread more rapidly (line 28). [1]
13. The history of sectarianism between the two groups of fans. [1] The tension that was building during the match. [1] The spectators rushing onto the pitch. [1]
14. a excited
    b When adding a suffix that starts with an 'e' to a root that ends in an 'e' [1], drop the final 'e' then add the suffix. [1]
15. The shirt [1]; the hat [1]; the scarf [1]; cheering when your team scores. [1]
16. The football team has experienced both success and failure [1], at times being in a high division and other times in a lower division. [1]
17. The statement is false. [1]
    Extract A states that football:
    - promotes healthy living and exercise (line 10) [1]
    - is a means of relaxation or relieving stress (line 9) [1]
    - is a social event because it is the 'most watched sporting event' [1]
    - is an inclusive sport followed around the world, 'more countries that are members of FIFA than there are countries in the United Nations'. [1]
    - Extract B mentions that footballers can be role models in society. [1]
    - Extracts C, '...next to that family just below us...' and 'D' 'My excited grandchildren...' show that it can be a family-centred game, enjoyed by all generations. [1]
    [1 mark for each of the following factors]
    - Stating own viewpoint clearly.
    - Including own knowledge.
    - Organising ideas into a logical structure.
    - Drawing ideas together into a summary or conclusion.
    - Good grammar, punctuation and spelling.

© Appendices

Practice Test 2

1 **b** [1] and **c** [1]
2 **a** When or just [1] **b** by [1]
  c great [1] **d** I or she [1]
3 Tattered pieces of wedding garments such as dresses and veils are on the floor. [1]
  Reference to the text: 'faded bridal relics', 'the other bridal wrecks'. [1]
4 **a** The shadows that the light casts over Miss Haversham make her look like an unreal, odd, unusual, mysterious or supernatural being. [2]
  b The damp, musty atmosphere was palpable or so strong it could be felt. [2]
  c The new day, daylight or dawn was noticeable in the sky (or coming through the window or curtains) providing some light. [2]
5 A candle holder [1] attached to the wall. [1]
6 **a** 'after beseeching Estella's attention to her' [1]
  b 'as of yore' [1]
  c 'It was the first time I had ever lain down to rest' [1]
  d 'designing to gain the outer court-yard' [1]
7 No, the writer is not enjoying his stay.
  [1] mark each for any five of the following points plus [1] mark for each text reference:
  - he has been trying to leave the room since he arrived; 'I took advantage of the moment – I had sought one from the first – to leave the room'
  - he didn't like looking at Miss Haversham; 'a miserable sight to see'
  - he was depressed as he walked around outside; 'It was with a depressed heart that I walked'
  - he stayed outside for over an hour; 'I walked in the starlight for an hour and more'
  - he was reluctant to return to the room; 'When I at last took courage to return'
  - he describes the evening as 'dragging on'; 'and so the evening wore away'
  - he couldn't sleep; 'A thousand Miss Havershams haunted me'.
8 **a–d** [1] mark each for any four of the following groups:
  whole/hole   I/eye   to/too/two
  heard/herd   saw/sore
9 [1] mark each for any eight of the following text references:
  - 'A thousand Miss Havershams haunted me'
  - 'I absolutely could no longer bear the place as a place to lie down in'
  - 'and walk there for the relief of my mind'
  - 'I saw Miss Haversham going along it in a ghostly manner'
  - 'making a low cry'
  - 'a most unearthly object by its light'
  - 'I felt the mildewed air'
  - 'never ceasing the low cry'
  - 'I tried in the dark both to get out, and to go back, but I could do neither'
  - 'I heard her footstep, saw her light pass above, and heard her ceaseless low cry'.
10 - Up to [3] marks for writing a sensible continuation that fits with the story so far.
   - Up to [2] marks for following the same style as the extract (similar choice of words, similar length of sentences, same scene and characters and so on).
   - [1] mark for writing within the word limit (130–150 words).
   - [1] mark for correct grammar and punctuation (the correct use of tense, starting each sentence with a capital letter and so on).
   - [1] mark for good overall spelling.

Practice Test 3

1 Line 2 states 'I sit in the top of the wood, my eyes closed.' This implies that the hawk is resting or roosting rather than flying. Explanation needed with reference to the text for mark to be awarded.
2 **a** *practise* [1]   **b** *branch, bough* [1]
3 This is a poem because:
  - it is written in six verses (stanzas) [1]
  - the lines are shorter than prose [1]
  - each line starts with a capital letter [1]
  - it uses punctuation to create rhythmic effects. [1]
4 The hawk is the narrator. [1] The text is written in the first person narrative, shown by pronouns that are used throughout, such as 'I sit'; '**my** eye'. [1]
5 Writing from the hawk's point of view allows the bird to be personified; giving it a voice so it can explain how it thinks and feels about its life. [1] This enables the reader to understand the bird's motivations and creates a more vivid reaction from the reader. [1]
6 **a** Tall trees are convenient for hawks and other birds, as the higher up a bird is, the more of the ground they can see. [1] This makes it easier to spot prey. [1]
  b Air currents make it possible for birds to 'float'. [1] A bird can move up and down with the changes in air pressure. [1]
  c The hawk is sitting on a branch with its feet 'locked upon the rough bark'. [1] As trees are part of the natural world, the hawk is holding Creation in its foot. [1]
  And:
  Hawks swoop down on their prey and grasp it in their talons. [1] As the hawk talks of death in the next verse, this phrase could refer to the creatures that it kills and carries with its feet. [1]

d 'Sophistry' means using false statements to deceive. **[1]** The hawk does not attempt to hide its motives or reason for being, as it is stating clearly that it is a bird of prey, designed to 'tear off heads' and to bring death. **[1]**

7 personification

8
- Sitting in tree tops enables a clear view of the ground below **[1]**; 'I sit in the top of the wood…' / 'The convenience of the high trees!' **[1]**
- Hawks can use air currents and the sunlight to help fly high above the ground and look for prey **[1]**; 'The air's buoyancy and the sun's ray/Are of advantage to me'. **[1]**
- The physical body of a hawk, with its beak and talons, is built for hunting and tearing flesh **[1]**; '… my hooked head and hooked feet'. **[1]**
- Hawks can judge their attacks well, flying straight for their prey **[1]**; 'For the one path of my flight is direct'. **[1]**

9
- regal **[1]**: feels like a king sitting 'in the top of the wood' **[1]**
- a perfectionist **[1]**: 'Or in sleep rehearse perfect kills and eat' **[1]**
- self-important, arrogant, feels in charge **[1]**: 'Now I hold Creation in my foot'; 'I kill where I please because it is all mine' **[1]**
- unemotional, matter-of-fact **[1]**: 'There is no sophistry in my body: /My manners are tearing off heads – '. **[1]**

10
- Up to **[2]** marks for a clear, structured argument and conclusion.
- Up to **[2]** marks for accurate spelling, punctuation and grammar.
- **[1]** mark for each individual, logical argument, which may cover points such as:

Agree with statement	Disagree with statement
They have large hooked beaks and talons, which they use to tear flesh as stated in the text.	They are beautiful, intelligent birds whose natural instinct is to kill in order to survive.
If there are many birds of prey in an area they could cause the decline of small mammal or bird populations.	Often wrongly accused of causing decline in bird and small mammal populations. Humans do far more damage by eroding habitats to build new roads, homes and so on.
They can be a danger to humans because they can cause serious damage with their talons.	If we didn't have hawks and other birds of prey, we could become overrun with rodents and other species of bird in urban areas as well as the countryside.
Prey has little chance to escape, as most hawks use the element of 'surprise' as their main attacking weapon.	They are victims and have been in danger of decline because of pesticide poisoning.
	All creatures have the right to life.

3 Additional resources

The **Bond** series offers extensive resources to support the development of your child's English skills:

- ✓ a complete course of workbooks that provide carefully graded, timed papers for extensive practice and revision
- ✓ mock test papers that present an authentic exam experience
- ✓ collections of short tests that offer essential bite-sized practice of all core skills
- ✓ tutorial guides that provide detailed strategies and practice activities for tackling all key topics and question types.

See the table below for individual title details.

BOND TITLES	ISBN
Assessment Papers in English 5–6 Years	978-0-7487-8464-6
Assessment Papers in English 6–7 Years	978-0-7487-8497-4
Assessment Papers in English 7–8 Years	978-0-7487-8105-8
Assessment Papers in English 8–9 Years	978-0-7487-8122-5
Assessment Papers in English 9–10 Years Book 1	978-0-7487-8112-6
Assessment Papers in English 9–10 Years Book 2	978-0-7487-8466-0
Assessment Papers in English 10–11+ Years Book 1	978-0-7487-8116-4
Assessment Papers in English 10–11+ Years Book 2	978-0-7487-8470-7
Assessment Papers in English 11+–12+ Years Book 1	978-0-7487-8483-7
Assessment Papers in English 11+–12+ Years Book 2	978-0-7487-8474-5
Assessment Papers in English 12+–13+ Years	978-0-7487-8478-3
11+ Test Papers in English (Standard)	978-0-7487-8488-2
11+ Test Papers in English (Multiple-choice)	978-0-7487-8487-5
10 Minute Tests in English 10–11 Years	978-0-7487-9697-7
How to do … 11+ English	978-0-7487-9695-3
The secrets of Writing	978-0-7487-8481-3
Get Ready for Secondary School: English	978-0-7487-7539-2
The Parents' Guide to the 11+	978-0-7487-9694-6

A full range of materials is also available to support verbal reasoning, non-verbal reasoning and maths practice.

Bond No Nonsense (BNN) is a home learning series for 5–11-year-olds that provides clear and straightforward teaching and learning of maths and English.

BNN English TITLES	ISBN	BNN English TITLES	ISBN
Ages 5–6	978-0-7487-9562-8	Ages 8–9	978-0-7487-9565-9
Ages 6–7	978-0-7487-9563-5	Ages 9–10	978-0-7487-9566-6
Ages 7–8	978-0-7487-9564-2	Ages 10–11	978-0-7487-9567-3

Schonell's Essential Spelling series offers the *Essential Spelling List*, which includes over 3000 words children often need to use in writing tasks, and three *Essential Spelling* workbooks for additional practice of keywords.

SCHONELL'S TITLES	ISBN
The Essential Spelling List	978-0-17-424493-6
The Essential Spelling Book 1	978-0-17-424083-9
The Essential Spelling Book 2	978-0-17-424082-2
The Essential Spelling Book 3	978-0-17-424081-5

For more details on any of these titles, please visit www.bond11plus.co.uk.